P9-ARD-899

# A New American Family

# A New
# American Family

*a love story*

## PETER LIKINS

The University of Arizona Press
Tucson

PROPERTY WLU
DISCARD
SOCIAL WORK LIBRARY

The University of Arizona Press
© 2011 Peter Likins
All rights reserved

www.uapress.arizona.edu

Library of Congress Cataloging-in-Publication Data
Likins, Peter W.
A new American family : a love story / Peter Likins.
p. cm.
Includes index.
ISBN 978-0-8165-2931-5 (cloth : alk. paper)
1. Likins, Peter W. 2. Adoptive parents—United States—Biography.
3. Interracial adoption—United States. 4. Families—United States.
5. United States—Race relations. I. Title.
HV874.82.L55A3 2011
362.734092—dc22
[B] 2010031369

Manufactured in the United States of America on acid-free,
archival-quality paper containing a minimum of
30% postconsumer waste and processed chlorine free.

16 15 14 13 12 11    6 5 4 3 2 1

To the heroine of our story,
the love of my life,
my wife and the mother of our children,
Patricia Likins

# Contents

# Illustrations

# Preface

When the polls closed on the West Coast on November 4, 2008, and the chorus of political analysts on television announced that Barack Obama had been elected president, I found myself sobbing uncontrollably.

Surprised by my own reaction, I later wondered why I was so moved by this decision of my fellow citizens. I am, after all, an old white guy, seventy-two at the time of the election, a straight, Catholic, former Republican trained as an engineer. John McCain was not only my senator from Arizona, he was then my respected friend. What powerful internal forces had pulled me into the Obama camp, despite all the stereotypes suggested by these labels I wear?

I had fully appreciated the intellectual appeal of Barack Obama's words in his two books and his many speeches. I agreed with his call for more civil (and civilized) public discourse and his fearless welcome of challenging ideas and ideals. I saw him as transcending the divisions that have polarized American politics, including race as well as party, looking beyond the petty conflicts of the moment to face the complex challenges of the future. But how did this election become for me such an emotional catharsis?

My wife, Pat, and I had raised six adopted kids in our multiracial family, but we had always insisted that we were not trying to change the world; we were only creating a beautiful family. Two of our children, like Barack Obama, were the product of black and white unions; two were Native Americans, one an Anglo child, and one of mixed Hispanic and Germanic American heritage. These racial and ethnic identities had been incidental to our adoptions; each of these children needed a family and we did too.

If race and ethnicity were so unimportant to me, why did I react so emotionally to the election of an African American president in the United States of America?

I have gradually come to understand that my commitment to my family has nurtured and been nurtured by my childhood belief that the ideals of the American democracy would someday be realized, the belief that someday people who look like my children would be accepted as just typical Americans, not set aside as "minorities." I had come to see our brood as a new kind of "all American family," born and raised in a changing America. But I was growing older and the time had not yet arrived when we would be perceived in America as simply Americans. The election of Barack Obama did not yet herald the arrival of that new day, but it made me believe again that my dreams for America and for future families like mine will be realized. Though that new day has not yet arrived, its dawning is now visible on the horizon for those who lift their heads high. The sense of relief in my heart and soul was just overwhelming. My tears were shed not for Barack Obama or even for my family; my tears of joy were shed for my country.

The discovery of that wellspring of emotions might have stayed within me, but something else was happening in my life. In April 2006 I sustained a life-threatening injury that sharpened my awareness of my own mortality. After my previously scheduled retirement as president of the University of Arizona at age seventy in July 2006, I felt keenly the need to record for family and friends my impressions of life's experiences, with special focus on family. Over the next two years I created a personal memoir to share my thoughts and feelings, generously illustrated with family photos. That book for family and friends was completed in 2008; I called it "In Darby's Eyes."

In the wake of the Obama election, I thought about the larger societal issues reflected in our experience of raising a multiracial family in America, and I began to wonder if there was a story of broader significance to be told. Is America ready to consider the possibility that in the course of the twenty-first century the American family will be a lot like mine?

Peter Likins
February 15, 2010

# Acknowledgments

My consultations with others in writing this book have been limited to occasional inquiries about specific issues and events, so the book's inevitable errors and omissions are my full responsibility.

I do owe a debt of gratitude to the good people associated with the University of Arizona Press, who guided me in the transformation of my personal reflections into a book that can reach beyond my own limited range to touch the lives of people I will never know.

# Introduction

If I had been a dreamer as a child, I would have dreamed the wrong dreams. I didn't have enough imagination to conceive of the wonderful life that has opened up for me, each chapter unfolding unpredictably over time. I didn't know enough about the world even to fantasize about the opportunities that would in fact be mine to explore. I didn't know enough about myself to see what others would someday see in me.

Perhaps most importantly, I didn't know that the beautiful stranger I boldly asked for a dance at my junior high school graduation party would become my life's partner, my best friend, and my accomplice in all of life's adventures. I was still thirteen; how was I to know? If Pat and I had not met in 1950 and married in 1955 at age nineteen, we would surely have missed the greatest adventure of our lives together: creating our multiracial family with six adopted children.

It was not uncommon for friendly observers to comment on our "international family." Always we were quick to correct them. Our children were all born in the United States of America. Ours is an all American family.

I will tell our story as candidly as a lifetime of disciplined honesty makes possible. Ours is not always a pretty tale and it is never a simple narrative, but it is a true story of an American family that speaks to the complexities of contemporary life in our country. I hope there is something of value here for every American and perhaps even for other citizens of the world who do not yet see clearly the American people as we are today.

Although this book is ultimately about our children, I must establish the foundations of our family by first introducing my wife and myself, Pat and Pete Likins. Because our work as teachers was inextricably intertwined with our lives as parents, I must describe our professional lives in parallel with our personal lives. I will tell our story retrospectively, looking back from the vantage point of the beginning of the Obama era, when in my early seventies I can pretend to the wisdom of advancing age without yet acknowledging fading memories.

# A New American Family

# Foundations

## Young Love

"Tonight I met the boy I'm going to marry." That's what my wife of more than fifty years wrote in her diary the night we met at my junior high school graduation dance in 1950. I was not yet fourteen, just barely bold enough to cross the dance floor to risk rejection by a new girl in school who was lovely to behold. I didn't have marriage on my mind.

We both sensed a special excitement as we danced throughout that evening, but we were just kids, living miles apart, and I was headed for a different school, so life unfolded separately for the two of us. I was just about to begin high school in Santa Cruz, California, where I would try out for the football and wrestling teams, determined to overcome the stigma of good grades by becoming "one of the guys" both athletically and socially. Pat came to high school a year later, finding her identity in music and theater, capturing the hearts of other boys. We both remember a high school dance when she was singing "Blue Moon" with the band and I was dancing with another girl, Pat and I each yearning for the other. In the year we finally came back together, Pat was elected to the cheerleader team and I was student body president and captain of the football and wrestling teams. We began "going steady" in that my senior year, both sixteen and very much in love.

When a full-cost academic scholarship made it possible for me to leave our hometown for college in nearby Palo Alto, we had an agreement that she could enjoy the social life of a popular senior girl and I could experience the excitement of my freshman year as an engineering student at Stanford. We went through the motions of separate lives, but this year apart merely strengthened the bond between us.

When Pat finished high school a year later and enrolled in a nursing program at San Jose State University, I spent the $250 I had received

*~ Pat and Pete at eighteen, engaged to be married (July 4, 1954).
(Family photo.)*

from the California Scholarship Federation for a quarter-carat diamond solitaire engagement ring, which I gave to my girl the night before my eighteenth birthday. When we married on December 18, 1955, we were both nineteen.

In those days a young man under twenty-one needed parental permission to marry in California. There was no father in my life, and my mom was understandably reluctant, fearing that I would never get out of college. I have a stark memory of our confrontation and my demand: "Mother, sign it!"

In retrospect my mother was right. I never did get out of college until I retired from my second university presidency, after forty-two years of faculty life and more than fifty years of marriage.

Although we didn't appreciate the significance of our declaration of independence at the time, Pat and I had already resolved at nineteen that together we would overcome the societal constraints and limitations that kept most people in their "proper place." I had been essentially self-sufficient since I graduated from high school at sixteen, supporting myself with scholarships and summer jobs, and Pat was equally independent. We were sure that we could stand on our own. We would follow our own hearts and minds wherever that might lead. We never imagined that our free spirits would lead us to six adopted children across the American spectrum of race and ethnicity, but the seeds of that adventure were already growing in our young hearts.

I realize that young people fall in love every day, and most often they drift apart (or race away from each other) when that passion is spent. Still, the excitement of young love is exquisite, with no parallel in the lives of mature adults. Many older people forget the overwhelming intensity of such emotions, which make everything else in the world fade into insignificance. Sadly, many older people have never experienced that kind of love and cannot fathom its power. But rarely does it survive the test of time. Rarely do the fiery passions of youth ignite the glowing embers of enduring love. When young love matures, however, it is extremely powerful. Our love continued to grow stronger over more than fifty years, building the foundation on which our family rests.

My wife and I often wonder why we were able to survive the stresses of early marriage, against all odds. We both were raised by strong, intelligent mothers with fine values, but we had little else going for us. We came out of what people then called "broken" families, impoverished, working-class folks with their full share of problems. We both entered adolescence with bundles of insecurities. Pat was moving from her Southern Baptist heritage to Catholicism, and my Protestant background was distinctly anti-Catholic. We knew, however, that we were two young people of very strong will with a deep commitment to each other and an unshakable determination to prove the doubters wrong. We really did believe that love conquers all.

## Family Roots and Branches

When Pat was thirteen she dropped a familiar, framed picture to the floor and broke the glass, only to discover as she rescued her baby photo from its frame that the inscription on the back identified her as Patsy Ruth Kitsmiller, a name she had never before seen or heard, born April 15, 1936.

Pat's mother, then known as Juanita Jolley, reluctantly revealed to her daughter the secret of her early marriage to Lee Kitsmiller, a man she had abandoned before she realized she was pregnant. She never told Lee about their child, but secrets don't remain buried in small Kansas towns, and Lee obtained a photo of Pat from the local studio where Juanita had taken her baby. He displayed that photo over his fireplace even after his second marriage and proudly claimed the daughter he didn't meet until she was twenty-four years old.

When Juanita married B. C. Jolley, Pat was almost three years old, having been nurtured by her grandmother for those precious years of infancy. Juanita and her new husband treated Pat as their own, and never told her otherwise. With no legal documents to make it official, she became Pat Jolley. When she stumbled across the truth about her birth from her photo in the broken frame, her mother extracted from her a promise not to let her daddy, B. C. Jolley, know about her discovery. Pat kept that promise until she was twenty-four, after she initiated contact with her birth father.

In complex ways, even at thirteen Pat felt liberated by her discovery, by the knowledge that she was not the birth child of a daddy who was too often violent and abusive to his four children and his wife. B. C. Jolley was a hard-working, hard-driving, hard-drinking man whose virtues included a gift for making music and a magical way with animals, but with other people he could be both difficult and dangerous.

Before the Jolley clan (Pat's daddy, his two brothers, and their father) settled in Scott's Valley near Santa Cruz, California, to establish a small business as road-building contractors, they had moved all over the American West, living in house trailers and following major highway construction projects from Texas to Washington. The Pacific Ocean halted a westward migration that began in the American South with prior generations, and the speech of the Jolley clan retained that voice.

Pat loved fiercely the three children born to B. C. and Juanita Jolley and she had a major role in raising them. Her little brother, younger by seven years, was born as Beverly Cooper Jolley, as was his father, and in time the boy was known as Bee. Sister Carol was nine years younger and little Barbara was eleven years younger than Pat. Juanita was an intelligent woman of exceptional warmth and affection, and as a fiery young woman she was compellingly attractive, but as her family grew and her problems compounded she seemed overwhelmed by her responsibilities. She relied increasingly upon her oldest daughter to maintain some sense of order in her crowded little two-bedroom house (with all four kids sometimes in one bed and always in one tiny bedroom). Pat emerged from this childhood environment with a fully developed sense of responsibility, which she regards as a gift from her mother.

When Pat was just seven years old, her mother left her in charge of her infant brother Bee in their house trailer. Although told to stay put, Pat left the trailer to go play with her friends. She felt responsible for the infant, so she took baby Bee with her. While they were gone the house trailer accidentally burned to the ground.

Pat's devotion to her brother Bee didn't end when she married me; Bee became my brother too. When he was fifteen, Bee was in trouble at home and needed a safe haven. Pat and I had just moved to Pasadena, after my graduate studies at MIT; I began work as an engineer with the California Institute of Technology at what became NASA's Jet Propulsion Laboratory (JPL) and she enrolled in Pasadena City College. Although Pat and I were just twenty-two, we welcomed Bee into our home and became for two years the de facto parents for young Bee. He was quickly surrounded by wonderful friends at Pasadena High, and they all made the Likins's apartment their favorite hangout. Bee was soon on a healthy path academically, athletically, and socially. His subsequent journey was not always an easy one, but he found his way to a successful military career, retiring after twenty years as an army major with a college degree, a wife, and three fine children. Bee likes to say that he absorbed life's most important lessons from his two years with us, illustrating with a simple story.

After some minor transgression at school, Bee conveyed to us the belief that it didn't matter because he didn't get caught. Apparently I hammered into his head the realization that what he had done was wrong even if no one knew about it but him. "Your sense of the kind of man you are comes firstly from within, so always behave honorably even if no one is watching." These words from a twenty-two-year-old surrogate father stuck in the head of a fifteen-year-old boy, never to be forgotten.

Pat's two sisters also found refuge in our home in times of need. When Carol suffered a bout of rheumatic fever in grade school her mother sent her to live with Pat and me in our tiny apartment at Stanford, knowing that Pat could care for her better than her mother could manage at that time. When Barbara's first husband was in Vietnam she shared our home and helped with our children, and again after she had a child of her own and that errant husband was gone.

Pat's experiences as a "mother" to her brother and sisters helped prepare her for the adventure that was to come with our own children. Very early on, she developed a high level of confidence in her ability to build a stronger family than she had known in her childhood.

Pat decided at a young age that she was going her own way, whatever the obstacles. Then she met me, and in time we discovered that we could go our own way together, marching in harmony to our own drummer.

Born on the Fourth of July in 1936, I was also one of four children (Tod, Pete, Jim, and Karen or "Katy" in sequence). When I met Pat in 1950, my mother was struggling to provide for her three sons in a two-room, cold-water cabin in the redwood forest outside of Santa Cruz, while baby sister Katy was in our grandmother's care in another town.

My mother, born as Dorothy Medlin, also married her high school sweetheart, a complicated young man who was called Bill Likins, although he was born as Ennis Blaine Darby. Bill had dropped out of school at fourteen and returned three years later, reemerging as a fine student, a good little football player (five foot two at best), and student body president at Tracy High in California. Dorothy was a lovely redhead, an excellent student, and secretary of the student body. When they married a year after high school, both had high potential but neither was prepared to make a living. In 1930 America was in the depths of the Great Depression.

Four children and hard times followed, exacerbated by Bill's preference for the neighborhood bar over either home or work. When his insubordination cost him a good job as a state-certified brand inspector in the stockyards, he continued to leave the house in the morning "for work" as usual, and his wife discovered that he was spending his days in the bar only when the anticipated paycheck failed to arrive. I remember vividly my parents exchanging blows when my father finally made it home that night.

Still, Bill was very proud of his boys and we loved our "Pop." I remember fondly the day Pop introduced my brother Tod and me to the boys at the bar, where the camaraderie was strong. I remember less fondly the many broken promises to take his boys to the rodeo or the wrestling matches, both his familiar haunts.

In early 1944, as the tide of battle in World War II was moving toward American victory, Pop left our family household in Hanford, California, and volunteered to join the navy. Only in retrospect did his wife and children realize that he had no plans to return after discharge.

Unable to pay the rent in Hanford, Mom took her brood (then one, three, seven, and barely nine years old) to live with her parents in Tracy to await her husband's return.

When Pop was discharged from the navy he visited his family in Tracy and told us to stay put until he got settled back in Hanford. I remember with anguish my fear of awakening Pop when he fell asleep on the couch with his head on my lap. I felt paralyzed with anxiety, afraid that I would lose my father if I disturbed his sleep.

Dorothy's mother and father (our "Nana" and "Da") managed somehow to accommodate their distressed daughter and her four little kids in their two-bedroom home for two years, my grades four and five in school. (I had skipped third grade in Hanford, thereby missing the introduction to cursive writing, plaguing forever my penmanship.)

When it finally became apparent even to my mom that her wayward husband was gone for good, she packed up her four kids and moved into a two-room cabin in the Santa Cruz Mountains that had long been in her family. For a year she did her best to make a home for her kids in that primitive cabin, but finally she had to get a job and find a way to care for her children while she worked (with Katy not yet in school). My mom got a job as a department-store clerk for $35 a week and began to build a new life with her boys in Santa Cruz, while Katy was sent back to live with Nana and Da.

Mom drove a few miles into town for work every morning, dropping her boys off at Mission Hill School, a functional combination of public elementary and junior high schools. I was the youngest and the smallest child in my sixth-grade class, and my insecurity as a new boy in school was further compounded by the realization that I was freckled, pudgy, and athletically inept.

Tod and I were in the same grade and just fourteen months apart in age, so we were often assumed to be twins. I think we had a kind of double impact on our classmates and teachers. We adjusted rapidly to our new environment, and by the time we were in our final year of junior high, Tod and I were elected as student body vice president and president, respectively. My confidence was growing, and I was bold enough at our graduation dance in 1950 to ask a pretty stranger to dance with me. I met Pat, and we have been dancing together ever since.

Just as Pat feels that she acquired her sense of responsibility from her mother, I have always felt that my frankly compulsive feeling of responsibility in all things I received as a gift from my father.

## Coming of Age

When my mother brought her children to live in the cabin among the redwoods a few miles north of Santa Cruz, she was taking them into an environment that was familiar to her from her own childhood. The Medlin family had for many years been escaping the summer heat of the San Joaquin Valley with brief visits to the redwood forests near coastal Santa Cruz, where relatives had a small cabin, and in 1936 my grandparents, Nana and Da, acquired a two-room tarpaper shack in this beautiful setting. The little community there, called Paradise Park, was established by the Masons in 1927, growing over time to include several hundred summer cabins owned by members of that organization. A few of those summer cabins had become permanent residences by the time my mother and her kids took refuge there in 1946.

The cabin enjoyed cold running water originating in Eagle Creek; we had an icebox in the kitchen and a toilet in a closet, but no bathtub or shower. The only source of heat was a large, wood-burning stove that served also as the only cooking appliance. Hot water was obtained from a big teakettle on that wood stove. We bathed once a week, or not at all when the river beckoned in the summertime. My mom was never a very large woman, but I remember well how difficult it was for her to squeeze into the galvanized steel washtub in the middle of the kitchen floor for her necessary bath.

A nearby utility pole brought a telephone line and electricity to the dwelling, powering a few wall sockets and the electric lights strung on open wires throughout the cabin. To make the place safer, my grandfather and his son Jim encased the wires in conduit. Eventually the woodstove was augmented by a coal oil stove for faster cooking.

The cabin was separated into two rooms by a partition that was slightly more than head high, with two curtained passageways connecting the two rooms. Members of the extended family had pooled their efforts to

~ *The cabin in Paradise Park.*
*(Family photos.) Above: Pete (left)*
*and Tod outside (c. 1943); right:*
*Pete at three (1939).*

cover the tarpaper exterior of the cabin with unpainted wooden shingles, leaving rough boards for the inside walls. There were gaps between those rough boards, so a pencil could be (and sometimes was) poked through the tarpaper from the inside, exiting to the open air between shingles.

Despite the improvements, conditions remained rather primitive. The cabin rested on four-by-four timbers lying directly on the dirt, rotting in the mud. The floor had caved in under the sink, so every ball dropped anywhere in the room rolled under the sink and disappeared. Mice took refuge in that same hole.

The cabin was augmented in later years and ultimately razed; no record exists that would document its dimensions. It may have been twenty feet wide by fifteen feet deep, with a front porch that provided sleeping space in the summer months.

Although the living conditions must have been very difficult for my mom, I remember my four years in Paradise Park as a time of positive and powerful formative influences in my young life. My mother might have wished otherwise, but her boys enjoyed almost complete freedom. We had learned to swim in the nearby San Lorenzo River, which became our natural habitat. We formed fast friendships with boys from other towns who came to Paradise Park every summer, and together we followed Eagle Creek or hiked up the river, sometimes diving for crawfish and boiling them alive in big pots on the beach, enjoying their meat by the fireside as much as I ever later in life savored lobster. We camped out all over the Santa Cruz Mountains, sleeping by our campfires under the redwoods, and in our teenage years drinking the beer that we labored to carry in our backpacks up and down those forested mountains. We were poor, I suppose, but nature is a great equalizer. The stellar jays who announced our presence among the redwoods didn't care whether we were wearing the favored Levi's or making do with jeans from "Monkey Wards" catalogs.

As kids we were vaguely aware of the pressures our mother bore, but only in retrospect can I fully appreciate the strength and courage she demonstrated in keeping our family from crashing during those challenging years in Paradise Park. Although we had little beyond life's essentials, we were never hungry or homeless. Equally importantly, she preserved in her children the fundamental values that were central to her family tradition, beginning with respect for education.

In my mother's generation, her working-class family culture denied girls the opportunity to go to college, but her brothers Bill and Jim both enrolled at UC Berkeley and ultimately earned, respectively, a Ph.D. in physics from Caltech and a master's degree in electrical engineering from Stanford. My mother's four children in their turn earned nine university degrees. We always knew that education was the path to a better life and we understood without words that our first obligation to the family's well-being was to do well in school. I don't recall ever being told to do my homework or study for a test; on the contrary, I remember my mother reassuring me that it was okay to bring home less than a perfect score on a test. (I misspelled the word "balloon" in the fourth grade and missed "business" in the sixth grade, failures of such magnitude that I remember them now, more than sixty years later.) The expectation that we would perform well in school was implicit in our developing sense of the need to meet our responsibilities.

We never doubted that our mother would find a way to keep us safe until we were ready to fly from our family nest. She managed, but not always easily.

There were no welfare payments coming in, no alimony, and very little, sporadic child support from Pop. When urged to pursue her kids' father for court-mandated child support, she'd say, "You can't get blood out of a turnip."

When little brother Jim and I needed tonsillectomies, my mom had neither health insurance nor money to pay for hospitalization and surgery. Doc Peterson gave us each a dose of ether and removed our tonsils in his office facilities. He expected no payment, nor did the dentist who routinely cared for our family.

Like other boys, Tod and I had odd jobs, such as delivering the *Santa Cruz Sentinel News*, raking leaves for other families, and caddying at Pasatiempo Country Club, an hour's cross-country hike away. Unlike other boys, however, we understood that any money we could earn went into the family cookie jar. We knew that our mom needed all the help she could get.

The Paradise Park boys sought out summer jobs we could do together. We tried our skill at picking strawberries, but most of us lasted only one day, developing a healthy respect for the adults working those fields, mostly Japanese Americans who did such stoop labor for a lifetime. (Actually I was the only boy who went back for a second day to help finish picking the field, earning even less than the $1.25 I received for my meager piecework compensation the first day.)

Our greatest adventure in working together was the summer we labored to load sixty-pound crates of pears for the Riske Trucking Company. (Yes, the name is pronounced as "Risky.") We had to move north to get these jobs, working in the hot sun all day and collapsing for the night in our sleeping bags on the garage floor of the trucking company. Our heroes were the truck drivers who manned with such skill their big Peterbilt and Kenworth rigs. At their most heroic, the truckers urged us to stay in school and prepare ourselves for a different kind of life than they were leading.

We also had great fun together, and sometimes got into trouble together. Deferring to a later chapter our escapades with alcohol, our crimes can be illustrated by a single tale: the great propeller heist at Bass Lake.

Among our summer buddies were two brothers, Joe and Bob Sand, the sons of a San Francisco plumbing contractor who was generous with his boys and their friends and seemingly endlessly wealthy. A few years after we moved into the cabin in Paradise Park, that good man and another family friend volunteered to build a sheet-metal stall shower by the toilet in our cabin, with water heater attached. His wife occasionally passed along needed clothing to the Likins boys.

When Tod and I went with a little gang of boys from Paradise Park on a camping trip to Bass Lake in the California Sierras, the Sand boys had a car and an outboard-motor boat sufficiently powerful to pull water skiers. I had no experience in handling a boat, but the Sand boys trusted me to make a run until I struck an object beneath the surface and broke the shearing pin holding the propeller in place. With the propeller at the bottom of Bass Lake, I felt responsible for ruining the trip for everyone.

A quick survey indicated that no compatible propeller could be purchased nearby, but a boat docked across the lake had an identical propeller. Although a number of the boys in that little gang had experience in petty thievery, they knew that I never stole anything. The responsibility was mine, however, and it was decided that I had to break my code and steal the propeller from the boat across the lake. Lacking the competence to remove the propeller underwater from a stationary outboard motor while treading water, I needed an accomplice. Another boy actually removed the needed propeller while I joined him in the water, carrying the tools and the getaway bag. Despite the cries of alarm emitted by a flock of ducks near the targeted boat, we escaped undetected and succeeded in our plan to recommission the Sand boys' boat.

When a young boy successfully steals one thing it can open the door to a lifetime of stealing, or it can create guilt that stills any future impulse to take something you haven't earned. I swam the seven-mile length of Bass Lake to expiate my sins, and never stole anything again.

On other fronts, too, I learned precious lessons of life during these four years of adolescent freedom in Paradise Park. Of course there were girls among the summer families in the Park, although we discovered them only as we entered our teenage years. Again, a single illustration makes the point.

During the summer of my thirteenth birthday, I became fascinated with an eighteen-year-old Japanese American girl who had come to the Park with a family who employed her to watch their children. Aiko and I spent many hours together, each learning from the other, sharing thoughts and feelings intimately. In our shared innocence our romance never crossed the lines of propriety that existed in those times, but the passion was a new experience for me. The fact that she was of Japanese descent seemed incidental at the time, but in retrospect I realize that this experience erased some cultural barriers in my mind.

Our years in Paradise Park came to an end just as Tod and I were completing junior high school. Our mother had found work first as a sales clerk at a department store and later as a clerk at a stationery and gift store owned and operated by Paul Forgey, a respected businessman in town whose daughter was enrolled in class with Tod and me and whose wife had recently died of heart failure. Over their several years together in the store, Paul and my mother developed a special relationship, although he was twenty years her senior. They married and the united family (including my little sister Katy) moved into a big house in Santa Cruz. With the financial pressures eased, we found that our new life offered many advantages, among them the freedom to participate in after-school sports as we entered high school. We realized even then, however, that we had been strengthened by our experiences in the beautiful but challenging environment of Paradise Park.

High school offered Tod and me the chance to test ourselves on the gridiron. Fortunately for us, Santa Cruz High had a "lightweight" football program for kids under 140 pounds, so we could learn the sport on our own terms. We were quick off the line but slow at 40 yards, and we had no ball-handling skills, so we began our football careers as scrub linemen, regularly getting beat up in practice by tougher, older boys and only occasionally playing in the interscholastic games. I was such a scrub I was assigned an old-fashioned leather helmet; I had to work hard to earn a modern plastic helmet like those worn by my teammates. I played left guard behind the starter, Billy Bell, who clearly enjoyed punishing me at every opportunity. I really didn't mind getting knocked around; I was happy just to be on the team.

The lightweight line coach, Jack Fiebig, recruited football players to start a new varsity wrestling team at Santa Cruz High. Tod and I had always enjoyed wrestling around on any available lawn, so we signed up. I quickly discovered that, although I could not beat my brother Tod, I could outwrestle the tough guys who had been pummeling me on the football team, including Billy Bell, who was widely regarded as dangerous. As I began to realize that I had unusual aptitudes for this sport, I began to see myself in a different light. Billy Bell treated me with new respect.

I lost my first wrestling match, pinned by John Deering of Salinas High in nine seconds, but I lost very few thereafter. Being pinned in wrestling is the ultimate surrender of control to an opponent, and I found that feeling of subjugation too devastating to ever repeat after that first match. In the seven years of competitive wrestling in high school and college that followed, I was never pinned again.

Five years later, as a junior in college, I was caught in a "cradle" by Robert Morgan of the San Francisco Olympic Club. With my knee jammed up against my nose and my back perilously close to the mat, I reacted like a desperate animal and broke Morgan's grip by straightening out my captive leg, breaking my ribs in the effort. I won that match, oblivious to my cracked ribs, but Morgan had prevailed when it mattered most, in the finals of the Far Western Championships the prior year.

Tod and I both had the kind of success in high school and college wrestling that redefines a young man's sense of himself. As a junior in high school (only my second year of wrestling) I placed second in the state tournament, and in my senior year I won the gold medal at 145 pounds and a little trophy as the tournament's "Outstanding Wrestler." Tod won the silver medal at 154 pounds, tied in an overtime match that was settled by the referee's (bad) decision. Coach Fiebig assigned these weight classes to my brother and me; either of us could (and sometimes did) wrestle at either weight. Our coach was strategizing for two gold medals, but in my family there were painful consequences. What would have happened if our weight-class assignments had been reversed?

Justice was served when Tod went to UC Berkeley and became captain of the Cal wrestling team, while I was Stanford's captain at a lower weight. We both earned silver medals in the Pacific Coast Conference as college sophomores.

In four years on the Stanford wrestling team, I never lost a dual-meet match for Stanford. I never had an undefeated year, however, because after the season was over and most teammates were gone I continued to test my skill in postseason tournaments, continuing until I was defeated (as I was eventually every year). I found this to be a very painful but effective way to preserve my humility.

✐ Wrestling. Left: Pete
at Stanford (1955);
below: Pete (left) and
Tod as wrestling captains
(1956). (Stanford Univer-
sity photos.)

Although Tod and I qualified for the National Collegiate Wrestling Tournament in our sophomore years of college, we were not able to afford the trip. I did receive national recognition, but not until 1993, when I was elected to the National Wrestling Hall of Fame in Stillwater, Oklahoma, admitted to the Hall of Outstanding Americans in the company of such luminaries as Abraham Lincoln, Teddy Roosevelt, and John Irving (my favorite author). I was proud to be recognized in such august company, but I would much rather have earned election to the Hall of Fame strictly as a wrestler.

In the culture of my high school, football was the premier sport, and it was not enough for me to excel in wrestling. Fortunately, I discovered that I could transfer my wrestling skills effectively to football, even on the varsity level against much bigger opponents. As a junior in high school I captained a league championship lightweight football team, earning "all-league" honors, and as a senior I was a very small varsity guard (just five foot five and 145 pounds), co-captain of the team, and honorable-mention all-league. We played both ways, offense and defense, in those days, with no face guards, and as a nose guard I took pride in the bruises and abrasions that I sported at the after-game dances. As a lineman, however, I rarely looked like a hero. Once, only once, did I have that chance.

Santa Cruz High School was expected to be crushed again in my senior year by archrival Watsonville High. But it rained and it rained until the field was a slippery bog under the players' cleats and our numbers were obscured by mud. Neither team could score, with superior punting by Santa Cruz balancing superior running by Watsonville.

As the time for the final whistle drew near, with Watsonville obliged to punt from deep in its own territory, I shot through the line and blocked that punt, sending the ball bouncing back through the end zone for a two-point safety. Watsonville was vying for a state championship, and lowly Santa Cruz won by two to zero. Amazing!

Even more amazing was the fact that I, Pete Likins, had for the first time in my life actually scored a point in interscholastic football. After this success, I knew that anything was possible.

The girl who became my wife soon after high school shared all my triumphs and matched them with her own. Pat came into high school carrying the burdens of a troubled home life, rebelling against a life defined by her daddy's family culture, and trying to find her own place in the sun. Pat was determined to go to college, although she knew that her dad would never countenance a liberal arts education for her. She got little encouragement at home; when her mother found time occasionally to help Pat with her math homework, she tended to do it rapidly for her rather than show her how to do it herself, further undermining Pat's confidence. In separating herself from her family culture, she was attending Catholic mass with her friends, well on her way to conversion with its implied rejection of her Southern Baptist heritage. (Actually Pat never rejected anyone's religion, but so it must have seemed to her Baptist family.) She was in a dangerous environment at home and Santa Cruz High School became her refuge.

Pat was an attractive, likable girl at school; just five feet tall and beautifully put together, she was never at a loss for a date. She incurred her daddy's wrath by going to the movies with a boy who was rumored to be of Cuban heritage, so she had to meet him secretly at the theater for the next date. Bobby Sakata was among her closest friends, although as a Japanese American he, too, would have stretched her daddy's tolerance. Cookie Barrientos, her very best friend, was an adorable girl with a vibrant personality and many friends, but Cookie struggled with her awareness of the prejudice that always threatened to greet the revelation that her birth father was Filipino. (Her own mother advised her to tell people she was Spanish.) Pat's love for Cookie helped her to build the moral foundation for the family we would later raise together.

Pat was blessed with a pure singing voice and a pure soul that kept her on her own true path. Mature beyond her years in every way, Pat met the challenges of her new environment with growing success. She was elected by the student body to the cheerleader team, was elected homecoming princess, and performed beautifully in musical and theatrical shows on campus. Most memorably, she did a routine with Rich Montgomery, a popular six-foot-six basketball star, who arose from a bench she had been circling, singing "I want to be loved by you," only at the end of the song. The audience roared with laughter when they realized that Rich towered over Pat by a foot and a half.

As her crowning performance, she was the soloist at her high school graduation, singing "Green Cathedral" to an appreciative audience.

When Pat and I began going steady, a popular cheerleader and the student body president and captain of the football team (and the wrestling team), we felt that we were on top of the world. We had no idea of the possibilities that lay ahead for us. We were just coming of age, just beginning to realize that we had a promising future together.

## Schools

### California Public Schools

We believed that the public schools in California's small towns were as good as any schools in America when Pat and I enrolled in those schools with our brothers and sisters. We benefited not only from dedicated teachers but also from our interactions with other kids from across the available social spectrum. When every kid in town goes to the same high school, the pool is as inhomogeneous as the town itself. By contemporary standards Santa Cruz was not very diverse; we kids caricatured our hometown as "a sleepy Italian fishing village" not without reason, but the concept of living and learning with the entire available youth population had value nonetheless. In that limited environment we learned to be comfortable with different kinds of people, lessons that would in time be applied to populations of much greater diversity.

Santa Cruz High School gave Pat and me the foundations we needed for further learning, both in college and in the harsher laboratories of life.

### Stanford University

Although Palo Alto was only thirty miles or so from Santa Cruz, I never allowed myself to think seriously about enrolling there. I thought Stanford was a place for rich, sophisticated families and my intention after graduating from high school at sixteen was to go out on my own, respectfully not burdening my mother and her new husband.

A very generous full academic scholarship offer and summer jobs made it possible for me to be a financially independent Stanford student. I was proud, but still scared. How would I fit in? Did I really belong in such an elevated atmosphere?

Twenty-five years after my Stanford graduation, I found myself welcoming a new class of equally scared freshmen to Lehigh University, where I was the new president. I wanted to reassure them but at the same time forewarn them that they should expect to survive some kind of setback during their first year of college, whether it was a bad grade, a dropped ball, or a lover's rejection. I wanted them to understand that almost every freshman encounters an acute disappointment in the first six months of college, but not every student has the self-confidence and emotional resilience required to bounce back from a bad day and go forward to a successful college career. I told them about my experience as a Stanford freshman:

> In the first of three quizzes in my freshman calculus class I got an A, although I was not comfortable with the material. When I got a B in the second quiz, I began to think that the entire class was even more lost than I was. On the third quiz I got an F! I had never seen an F before, and I was devastated by the grade. That same day I got beat up in the wrestling room by a teammate from Pennsylvania and I had a fight with my girl. My world was falling apart in just one day.
>
> But here I am, in fine robes on the platform before you as your university president. I survived. In fact I earned a B in the class, I made the wrestling team and I married the girl! If I can do it, you can too. So when the sky is falling on your head, try to remember: You can take a blow and still excel in this university.

This story was not the most significant of my Stanford memories, but it proved to be useful for fifteen years in the Lehigh University presidency and for another nine years in the presidency of the University of Arizona. Alumni came back years after graduation with sharp memories of my freshman story, which made a difference for them. They could identify with their president as a human being, and that gave them the confidence to go forward, even against the wind.

All Stanford freshmen lived on campus in residence halls in those days, and I lived in Encina Hall. I kept a giant photo of Pat in a bathing suit on my wall, matching any pinup in Encina. I studied hard and kept up with my work, so when finals came I could set my worried mind at ease with a light novel (Perry Mason mysteries were preferred), get a good night's sleep, and relax in preparation for the stresses of the exams. When my friends were pulling all-nighters to prepare for exams, I pursued a different strategy. This worked for me throughout my university years; never did I study through the night.

Pat graduated from high school as I concluded my freshman year at Stanford. We celebrated in July on the night before my eighteenth birthday by becoming engaged to be married. Pat enrolled at San Jose State University to earn her nursing degree, but the impatience of youth brought us together during that first year. We got married on December 18, 1955, in the middle of my junior year. The day before our wedding

*⮜ Pat at twenty (1956). (Family photo.)*

I completed three final exams at Stanford, trying for eight hours to concentrate with my mind elsewhere.

Disneyland opened in Anaheim in 1955 and that became our honeymoon destination. We were still kids at heart, even as we faced the world as a married couple at nineteen. We celebrated our fiftieth wedding anniversary at Disneyland, which was, of course, celebrating its golden anniversary as well. The management made the most of their special guests, providing a magnificent suite at the top of the Disneyland Hotel.

With some hesitation, I participated in fraternity rush in the spring of my freshman year, accepting a bid from Delta Tau Delta. I realized only later that my new brothers found my ducktail haircut and my attire a bit strange, as my only suit was light blue with pants pegged at the ankles and a "one button roll" jacket that hung very low. With the addition of my looping gold keychain and blue suede shoes, I was simulating the zoot-suit look of that era, I suppose, but in my small-town culture this look was cool. My new brothers accepted me anyway, and in time they embraced Pat as well. I was elected president of my pledge class.

It troubled me even as a freshman, and much more later, that most national college fraternities were then restricted to Caucasian, Christian males. My brothers at Stanford shared my disdain for the national fraternity policies, which we challenged in ways that seem tame by the standards of the sixties but seemed quite brave at the time. We welcomed two Jewish brothers into the house, but we didn't inform the national headquarters. We initiated a Samoan student into the fraternity, standing our ground when the national officers protested that he seemed darker in his pledge class photo than most African Americans. A member of my class, Hap Wagner, led an early attempt to persuade the national fraternity to change its policies, planting seeds that grew into challenges that eventually changed fraternity policies nationwide. Delta Tau Delta is now proudly inclusive and admirably honorable in its policies, but not so in the 1950s.

Hap Wagner became a very successful corporate executive as CEO of a multibillion-dollar global chemical company, but like me he came from modest circumstances, entered Stanford as an engineering student on a scholarship (basketball), and married his college sweetheart (Marcia). Pat and I admired Hap and Marcia greatly, and we were pleasantly surprised when decades later, by remarkable coincidence of our professional paths, our two families became residents of Bethlehem, Pennsylvania, in the Lehigh Valley. Hap had served as an usher in our wedding, and thirty years later Hap and Marcia escorted us down the aisle of another church as we celebrated our thirtieth anniversary by renewing our vows.

I majored in civil engineering at Stanford, plunging straight ahead toward a goal I had set for myself at age ten and pursued in summer jobs with my survey crew lineman experience at fifteen and subsequent labor in road construction. The curriculum for engineering students is closely prescribed, even in such a fine university as Stanford, and I followed the requirements, performing very well in my classes. My pleasure in learning, however, was most intense in the study of history, English, and philosophy. In my final quarter of study at Stanford, I asked my advisor to approve courses in philosophy and American literature, shocking the good man, who assumed that I would want to take more math and engineering courses to better prepare myself for the coming challenge of graduate school. He relented, and I enjoyed two of the most important courses of my undergraduate experience. In my course on twentieth-century American literature I was the only student not majoring in English, and my classmates earned my respect by demonstrating that there is more than one way to excel intellectually.

Despite these impulses toward the humanities, I continued on the straight path to my goal of becoming an engineer. I was not yet twenty-one when I claimed my bachelor's degree in civil engineering at Stanford. As graduation approached, I began job interviews, torn between Bechtel Construction and a job as a structural engineer in the aircraft industry. Pat and I enjoyed being together in marriage and both dreamed of raising a big family on an engineer's salary. However, several faculty members urged me to apply for graduate school, which would require fellowship support. With Pat's encouragement, I applied for admission and a fellowship at five graduate schools, seeking a master's degree. (Pat later admitted that she feared my excitement about a business law course would draw me into law school, which would have taken three years rather than the single year minimally required for a master's degree. Neither of us imagined that my engineering education could continue beyond the master's level.)

I was deeply honored to receive a fellowship from the national engineering honor society, Tau Beta Pi, funded by the Honeywell Corporation and applicable to any university in the country. MIT added a tuition scholarship to the fellowship, covering all costs, and I chose to go to MIT. I left Stanford a very different person than had entered four years earlier.

### Massachusetts Institute of Technology

When Pat and I drove our old Ford all the way to Boston in 1957, we knew that we were about to enter an entirely new world and felt incredibly brave to be out there on our own. That old car coughed and stuttered all the way across the country, but we got there on schedule. We found a single room to rent on Commonwealth Avenue in Boston, sharing a bathroom with our neighbor the dentist and all his patients during the day and paying twice the rent we had been paying for married student housing at Stanford. Rather than pay extra to park our car in the alley behind the apartment, we removed the battery and stored the car in a lot out of town, hoping it would come back to life when we needed it to drive home in the spring. I walked across the Massachusetts Avenue Bridge to MIT for class and Pat walked to her clerical job nearby. We were ready for anything.

Going to graduate school at MIT was heady stuff for me. In my mind, MIT was the pinnacle of engineering education in the entire world, and yet I was there. Moreover, from the Cambridge perspective I could see Stanford more clearly, and only then did I realize that Stanford, too, was among the world's best engineering schools. From my perspective in Santa Cruz High School, I knew that Stanford and Cal were the finest universities in Northern California, but I had to move to the East Coast to discover that they were among the finest universities anywhere. This discovery recalibrated my sense of myself; I now knew that I was playing with the big boys and winning the game.

I completed my master's degree at MIT in nine months of intensive study, finding time to explore Boston's rich cultural palette with Pat as two excited youngsters. We had very little money, but Boston can be explored on foot and by subway, so we never felt that our opportunities for enrichment were being denied. Our enthusiasm for Boston has never faded.

At MIT my academic interests were expanding beyond my mainstream civil engineering courses. When Sputnik I was launched by the Soviet Union in October 1957, I was shocked by the realization that a man-made satellite could be placed in orbit around Earth. In an advanced dynamics course at Stanford one year earlier I had correctly solved a problem in our textbook, joining my classmates and my professor in demonstrating that this feat was infeasible; we all assumed a single-stage rocket, which would have to be of skyscraper proportions just to place a pea in orbit. On January 31, 1958, the United States used four rocket stages to launch the Explorer 1 satellite, developed by the Jet Propulsion Laboratory (JPL) of the California Institute of Technology. JPL has been operating under exclusive contract with NASA since that space agency's official creation on October 1, 1958, but prior to that time JPL was operating under contract with the army.

I was primed to be swept off my feet by the JPL recruiters who came to MIT in the spring. After pursuing a singular goal of becoming a civil engineer since I read a book about the Panama Canal in the sixth grade, and achieving a master's degree in the subject, I abandoned that earthbound career path and jumped into space.

## California Institute of Technology

I was not a student at Caltech; I was employed off campus at JPL as a development engineer, working on new Earth satellites and space probes. Nonetheless, I thought more deeply about the foundations of engineering during my two years at JPL than in the course of completing my classes at MIT and Stanford. The space environment differs from the terrestrial environment in ways that invalidated some of the unspoken premises of my Earth-centered civil engineering education, but I had no way of knowing that except by thinking on my own more critically than ever before. There were no textbooks from which to learn about space exploration and no experts to turn to. There were no degrees in spacecraft engineering or aerospace engineering; we were an eclectic combination of scientists, mathematicians, and engineers of all stripes, trying to figure out together what to do next. I was incredibly fortunate to be working as an engineer in the very first year of human exploration of space.

When I left MIT for JPL, I knew that this was to be no more than another stage of the journey that had by that time been defined in my mind. I wanted to become a college professor, and that meant going back to school for my doctorate. I needed a couple of years to get some practical experience as a real engineer, recoup our finances, and give Pat the opportunity to recommence her own education at Pasadena City College, hoping that we could both continue our university studies somewhere after two years in Pasadena.

## Pasadena City College

When we moved back to California and I finally had a real job, it was Pat's turn to be a full-time student. Nearby Pasadena City College was a promising point of reentry for Pat, who decided that she wanted to qualify as an elementary school teacher. Without changing her goal, she soon changed her academic major to English, with a minor in Spanish, finding more substance in these courses and more stimulus from the faculty. For the first time in her life, Pat was in an environment that supported her academic aspirations, and she flourished as an honor student in Spanish with excellent grades in all her courses. After two years she qualified for transfer to Stanford.

Family always came first for Pat and me, and, as noted previously, we didn't hesitate to welcome Pat's brother Bee into our household when he needed refuge. In our two years together, Bee Jolley became an important presence in our memories of Pasadena.

## Stanford Together

When Pat and I returned to Stanford in 1960, we both enrolled as students. I had a Ford Foundation fellowship for my Ph.D. studies, including a stipend, free tuition, and a loan that was to be forgiven if I became a professor upon graduation. We paid Pat's tuition until, predictably, the money ran out and she had to drop out again to keep me going.

I was shifting from my previous major in civil engineering to the field of engineering mechanics, which establishes the foundations on which other engineering disciplines are constructed, committing myself to research in spacecraft dynamics.

Pat continued her studies in English and Spanish, enjoying simply being a successful Stanford student, learning from distinguished faculty in that rarefied environment. Her gift for languages was exceptional even at Stanford.

We were both sufficiently mature to understand the value of learning for its own sake, and not merely as a means to an end (which for us as kids was simply employment). At the same time, we were more than ready to conclude our schooling and start a family. We adopted our first child even before I graduated.

Although my JPL experience had sharpened my interest in the advanced study of dynamics for application to spacecraft, I developed confidence in my ability to master the complexities of this field only when a young professor of dynamics named Tom Kane joined the Stanford faculty. He demystified the kinematics underlying dynamics with formal analytical constructions based on vector calculus, and I developed an approach to this work that served me well for decades to follow. Teachers really do matter.

I completed my dissertation under Tom Kane and joined the UCLA engineering faculty in 1964 as an acting assistant professor (earning half the pay that I was offered by the Hughes Space Systems Division in Southern California). After almost nine years of marriage, I had what I hoped would be a permanent job. With our new baby, Pat and I were ready to face the world.

### California State University, Northridge

As I progressed through the academic ranks at UCLA and our family grew to include four adopted children, I really believed that our years of university education were over, but Pat was still hungry to complete her degree. To my surprise, with four kids in tow (sometimes literally), she enrolled at age thirty-four in nearby Cal State Northridge, finished her degree in English in 1973, and then continued with graduate studies to qualify as an elementary school teacher in 1974, realizing the goal she had set for herself sixteen years earlier. We had adopted two more children in 1972, while Pat was in school, so she finally graduated as the mother of six. I was very proud of my wife.

I was also proud (but less surprised) when she reported with some embarrassment that a young male student on campus had looked her up and down and exclaimed, "Strictly voluptuous!"

## Teachers

With no father in my life and a mother with many conflicting responsibilities, I accepted the guidance of devoted teachers to an extraordinary degree. From grade school through grad school, my personal and professional development has been profoundly influenced by teachers. My debt to them could be repaid only by teaching others as they taught me.

My early decision to become an engineer was stimulated by teachers in the sixth and seventh grades, although they could not have known their influence. My sixth-grade teacher, whom I remember only as Miss Janes, gave the class an assignment to write about what we would do when we grew up. I had just finished a book about the career of George Washington Goethals, the civil engineer who completed the Panama Canal, so of course I wrote about my plans to become a civil engineer. The next year a different teacher gave her class the same assignment, so of course I handed in the same essay. The die was cast.

Billie Hunkin was the school librarian at Mission Hill School in Santa Cruz when I began there in the sixth grade, and she took me and my brother Tod under her capacious wings for the four years we were enrolled there. She was always seeking out students with high potential, administering individual IQ tests to selected students to that end. (At 152 I was her top scorer at a time when the silliness of any scalar measure of intelligence was not as obvious as it is today.) Under Miss Hunkin's tutelage, I read books in a carefully structured progression, starting with stories about horses (by Will James) and dogs (by Jack London) and then advancing through the classics by Victor Hugo, Alexander Dumas, and Charles Dickens, all extracurricular reading beyond school assignments.

Miss Hunkin also helped me gain confidence in public speaking. One such instance comes especially to mind. Wearing pants low on the hips is not just a twenty-first-century fashion; Levi's were also dangerously low in 1950. The principal of Mission Hill, Sam Reed, felt the need to intervene personally, but Miss Hunkin had a better idea. She challenged me in my role as student body president to tell my classmates during the next school assembly to pull up their pants. This was a delicate assignment, so I enjoyed the look of surprised amusement in my mentor's eyes when I said to my classmates, "Pull up your pants. Your epidermis is hanging out."

Most important to my early language development was a ninth-grade English teacher named Mabel Fitzgerald. She was equally influential with my brother Tod and a year later with Pat, who became an English major in college. Miss Fitzgerald was a tough, feisty lady and she taught the English language the old-fashioned way, emphasizing the diagramming of sentences. Throughout a lifetime of written and oral communications, I have automatically diagrammed sentences in my head. When people occasionally comment on my penchant for speaking extemporaneously in proper sentences, I always give credit to Miss Fitzgerald.

Although my love of language has always been central to my intellectual life, in high school my focus shifted to math and science. I wanted to become an engineer and I discovered that I could excel in these critical fields. A key influence in this developing interest was Alpheus Green, an intellectual of high order who presided over advanced mathematics at Santa Cruz High. He taught mathematics with precision and utter clarity, setting a high standard for me to emulate many years later.

In some ways the most important teacher in my young life was my high school wrestling coach, Jack Fiebig. I'm sure I needed a father in my life, and Jack Fiebig filled that void better than anyone. One of the most important lessons he taught me had nothing to do with wrestling. Mr. Fiebig also taught mechanical drawing, in which class I earned a B that blemished an otherwise perfect, straight-A record at a time when that was the highest grade given. I did not become class valedictorian because my wrestling coach gave me the grade I deserved in mechanical drawing, setting aside the fact that I was his star performer on the mats and a state champion. He played it straight, with no quarter given to favorites.

In my freshman year at Stanford I discovered a new and exciting way to learn. Every Stanford freshman in those days was obliged to enroll in a class on the history of Western civilization, meeting each week in a large auditorium for one grand lecture followed by three meetings in sections of thirty or so to explore readings and engage in discussions. Examinations were conducted in the classroom setting, but, in conformity with the Stanford Honor Code, without faculty or grad students walking the room to prevent cheating.

After one quarter of the three in the typical Stanford academic year, one or two students in each section were invited by the presiding section professor to forgo the usual format and pursue the balance of the year's study of "Western Civ" in a group of four or five selected students meeting one evening a week with the professor in his lodgings to discuss a much expanded curriculum with prodigious reading assignments. For the next two quarters my peers and I met with young Professor Kaminsky of the Philosophy Department to delve deeply into Western civilization history as it unfolded over time. Professor Kaminsky became a persuasive advocate of every new idea as it was introduced historically, leaving it to his students to think critically about his arguments. This was an entirely new way to learn for me and my classmates in this honors course, and we all found it immensely stimulating.

Although every weekly meeting with Professor Kaminsky had the tenor of an oral exam, there were no formal tests until the final exam and no grades were given until the end of the year, when we had two quarters of credit at stake. When we showed up for the final, Professor Kaminsky handed out the assignments and told us to take the exams back to our dorm rooms and work in solitude, with books closed, returning in two hours. I cannot imagine anyone who is vested with such trust to betray that trust by cheating.

Fifteen years later, when I was a young professor at UCLA, an undergraduate in a large dynamics class came to me the day after an exam and apologized for missing the test due to illness, expressing the hope that a makeup exam could be administered. I asked him if he had seen yesterday's exam or discussed it with anyone. He had not. I handed him the same exam and told him to be back in an hour with the test completed. UCLA did not have an honor code and cheating was not unknown even when testing was monitored closely. But this young man came back to my office an hour later with a completed exam that was typical of his work, almost in tears as he assured me that he could never violate such a trust. I taught him more than dynamics that day.

The teachers who shape our minds early in life are often more powerful in their influence than college professors can be, especially for undergraduates. Pat encountered an important exception late in her educational journey when, at age thirty-six, she took an undergraduate math class at Cal State Northridge from Professor Viggio "Pete" Hansen. Like many young girls with inadequate preparation and unsupportive parents, Pat grew up anxious about mathematics. For her teaching credential at Cal

State Northridge Pat needed a math class, and she fearfully dropped the first one she tried. When she enrolled in Pete Hansen's class, which began with binary number systems and ranged widely, he made her realize that she has a real aptitude for the subject. Pat has always possessed an uncanny ability to recall numbers and she has always been proficient with arithmetic, but she didn't connect any of this with the mysteries of higher-order mathematics. Pete Hansen helped her to make the connection by taking some of the mystery out of mathematical theory. Once her inhibitions had been banished, Pat took pleasure in teaching mathematical constructs such as maps and other graphical representations to children, building mathematical foundations at an early age. When Pat plunged into the world of digital photography and personal computers decades later, she tackled the challenges of teaching herself new skills with verve and confidence. Teachers really do matter at every level.

By the time Pat realized her aspiration to be an elementary school teacher, she was already a seasoned teacher of her own six children and the children previously in her care, starting with her siblings and including five preschool children she cared for in our married-student housing community at Stanford when our funds for her tuition were exhausted. She was able to get a job teaching the third grade in the parochial school where all six of our children were enrolled, with a Likins child in six of the eight grades of that school and Pat in another. She had discovered a unique way to stay close to her kids and realize her ambition to teach school at the same time.

My own undergraduate education at Stanford was profoundly influenced academically by many professors who were excellent teachers. I revered my faculty and treasured the opportunity to learn at their feet, but I saw myself in such a way that I could not relate to them as regular people like me. They seemed somehow elevated beyond my reach as a human being, although I excelled as a student. As a Stanford senior with top grades and a fellowship for graduate study at MIT, I was approached after class in the hall by a favorite professor, Donovan Young, who was also my faculty advisor, with the totally unexpected question: "Have you ever considered becoming a professor?" It had never before occurred to me that such an exalted role might be possible for me, but I never forgot the question.

My thesis advisor at MIT, Dr. Charles Norris, was able to break through the barrier that separated me in my mind from the ranks of college professors, and it is to Chuck Norris that I owe my decision to pursue my doctorate in the hope of becoming a professor. He allowed me to see him as a human being, a man who shared his concerns about raising his son and protecting his family. He reached into my soul to stir new dreams.

Finally, the strongest influence on my intellectual grasp of the disciplines of kinematics and dynamics that would become the foundations of my own faculty life, and the most important contributor to my skills as an engineering professor, was my Ph.D. advisor at Stanford, Tom Kane.

Although my own professional life has included years as an engineer and college professor, dean, provost, and president, in my heart I have always been a teacher. My own kids can attest to that, as can hundreds of youngsters Pat and I coached when our children were involved in youth sports in New Jersey. Even as a university president I worked hard to be an effective mentor for students, faculty, and other officers of the universities I served. I even tried to teach our legislators, with less success.

I have always regarded teaching as the noblest of my professional endeavors, even as my own work drew me first into research and then into administration. I enjoyed the role of Ph.D. dissertation supervisor at UCLA and Columbia, combining as it does both teaching and research. As a dean, provost, and president I always found time for students, whether teaching a class or guiding student body presidents. I'm not at all sure that I ever became very good at being a boss, but I know I was a good teacher.

More challenging in my mind than any of these roles is being a good parent. Teaching, guiding, mentoring, and advising are all important responsibilities for a parent, but wholly insufficient for the role. When teaching becomes pedantry, parenting dies. Something more than teaching is needed, and the balance of this book is an exploration of those ephemeral qualities that make up a true family.

# 2

# Kids

## Stanford Village

Military hospital barracks hastily constructed near Stanford University during World War II were transferred after the war to Stanford University and used in part for the Stanford Research Institute and in part for "Stanford Village," housing married students. Soon after our marriage Pat and I rented a tiny gingerbread house in a Stanford neighbor's backyard, where we lived until a Stanford Village apartment opened up for us. We enjoyed our first home together in that adorable little playhouse, which had a single bed that served as a couch in the "living room" (the only real room) and a kitchen that was so miniature that my diminutive wife could stand in one place and touch all four walls and the ceiling. We felt isolated, however, despite visits from fraternity brothers (who were obliged to duck their heads to enter the front door), so we were elated to move into a community of students at Stanford Village who shared our life experience. Our neighbors were mostly graduate students, some from other countries, so we learned from them as well. Our rent was $45 a month.

Three years later, when Pat and I returned to Stanford, this time both as Stanford students, we were pleased to move back into Stanford Village. This time we were in a unit that had been part of the psychiatric ward in the old military hospital, so the windows were clouded and enmeshed with chicken wire. We suspended perforated wallboard panels from the ceiling and built bookcases of bricks and boards to fabricate "rooms" for sleeping, cooking, and studying, creating a functional and quite livable home for the next four years.

Pets were forbidden in Stanford Village, but the cloudy windows made detection of our tiny Siamese cat (Tuptim) unlikely, and at times we stretched the rules a bit further. We rescued a lost German shepherd on a busy freeway (the "Bloody Bayshore") and he lived with us until we were able to find a more appropriate home. We rescued Troubles, a very pregnant stray cat who came to our door in a rare Palo Alto snowstorm. We intended to keep Troubles in our sheet-metal-lined shower only until she had her seemingly imminent kittens, but as the days went by (without showers) Pat realized that veterinary intervention was required to save Troubles and her brood. An episiotomy solved that problem but created another as we struggled to pay the vet's fees. Troubles and her surviving kittens joined our family, as about a hundred other pets of great variety have done in the course of time.

As much as we loved our animal friends in Stanford Village, we treasured even more our relationships with our neighbors and their children. Next-door neighbors from Jamaica became lifelong friends and ultimately godparents of one of our children. When we ran out of money for Pat's tuition and she had to postpone her degree again, two Japanese American families from Hawaii asked Pat to provide daily home care for their children, five in number. Pat and I both fell in love with those adorable kids, who found a special place in our hearts. We knew then that we could love these children as our own and this realization made our later commitment to adoption an easy decision.

We adopted our first child before I finished graduate school at Stanford, making room for her bassinette in what had been a study alcove in our Stanford Village apartment. Stanford Village was our daughter Lora's first home.

## Children

Because going to college full time occupied either me or Pat or both continually for the first nearly nine years of our marriage, we accepted the need to wait more than seven years for the children we desired, waiting until I approached the end of my graduate studies with a real job in the foreseeable future. As that time approached, however, we experienced several early-stage miscarriages, which threatened our plans for a large family; we wanted at least to match the four children in Pat's childhood and mine. Having children is not important for everyone, but for Pat and me this experience seemed to be an essential element of a fulfilling life.

For Pat, the need for children was compelling. Pat had been a surrogate mother to her younger siblings since she was a child herself. Her love for the children of other families as she cared for them in Stanford Village was beautiful to see but hard to watch as I began to fear for our own prospects for childbirth. Pat wanted to teach in elementary school because she loved small children and knew they would love her too. My wife simply had to become a mother.

In a way that I find hard to explain, raising children was not only an emotional need for me, it was an important life experience that I didn't want to miss. Perhaps because my own father had abandoned his family responsibilities when I was a child, I felt a powerful need to assume such responsibilities myself, as though I needed to prove to myself that I was worthy of fatherhood. I wanted to be there for my children, teaching them to swim or ride a bike, lessons I had to learn for myself. I wanted them to have more practice in catching a ball or looking under the hood of an automobile than I ever had, hoping that my children would develop skills that I never mastered. (I hadn't figured out how I would teach them what I didn't know!) I wanted to cherish hugs when they woke up in the morning and tuck them into bed at night.

I also wanted to give my dear wife the children she needed and deserved. I knew that Pat would be a very good mother, loving her children dearly and at the same time capable of the organization and direction of their development that seemed mysterious to me. Having prospered in a childhood almost totally lacking in discipline, I knew that I was not well prepared for disciplining my own children, but I was prepared to follow my wife's lead and learn how to be a proper parent.

I was ready and she was ready, but the opportunity for us to bring children into the world together seemed to be slipping away.

## Adoption

Should we be thinking about adoption? We both knew that we could love children not born to us, and we understood too that even biological offspring don't come with any guarantees.

I had been carrying around in my head since I was a seventeen-year-old Stanford freshman the admonitions to parents expressed by the Lebanese-American poet Kahlil Gibran in a 1923 publication called *The Prophet*. He reminded us all that we don't own our children, that they are instead "the sons and daughters of Life's longing for itself."

I was not so far removed from childhood myself when I first read *The Prophet,* and perhaps I read the poem from the perspective of the child, not the parent, but these words were etched indelibly in my mind.

Of course, Gibran was speaking through the Prophet to parents who create their own children, and that's the way I read him in 1953. The message to adopting parents is, however, even more powerful: What is obviously true for parents of adopted children is also true for parents who give birth to their own. In either case, your children "are the sons and daughters of Life's longing for itself."

Kahlil Gibran wrote *The Prophet* in 1923. Although the nature-versus-nurture debate was raging in scientific circles even before Francis Galton coined the phrase in 1874 and modern concepts of genetics had been developed in the very early 1900s, it seems unlikely that Gibran was influenced by either the science or the pseudoscience of his times. Certainly he had no knowledge of the DNA molecule, whose structure was determined in 1953, or of the assemblies of DNA called genes. Gibran was using the language of poetry to tell us as parents that we cannot expect to fully control the nature or the development of our children. He spoke with the wisdom of the poet.

If Gibran were to speak to us in the twenty-first century in contemporary language, abandoning the mood of the poet, he might tell us that in the raising of children, biology trumps sociology. Children are brought into this world because of the biological need to procreate the species, not just in order to provide parents with an opportunity to establish family units of their own creation. This message is delivered today not by poets but by biologists and their translators.

Thanks to such popular writers as Matt Ridley, it is now widely understood that "nature versus nurture" is the wrong debate. Ridley's concept, delineated in his books *Genome* and *The Agile Gene*, is "nature via nurture," a phrase intended to convey current understanding that the assembly of genes with which we are conceived interacts with environmental influences, which switch on and off the genes that provide instructions for the body's manufacture of the protein molecules that ultimately shape our bodies, including our brains.

The twenty-first century is already a time of impressive progress in scientific understanding of the functions of various parts of the human brain, in large part because of the dramatic development of noninvasive brain-imaging technologies. More invasive exploration of the functioning of the brains of other animals has also accelerated our understanding of our own brains. We now know that certain fundamental brain functions, including the capabilities associated with human attachment, develop very early in childhood or not at all. As our knowledge of brain development continues to expand, there will be lessons learned that are particularly important to parents of adopted children. Some prospective parents will be discouraged by the realization of the magnitude of their challenge and others will function more effectively because of their deeper understanding. Social workers will see their responsibilities more clearly and recognize the urgency of getting infants into adopting families as soon as possible. The world of adoption will get better, but more complex.

The six children who were ultimately adopted into our family were all born in the 1960s, at a time when the old nature-versus-nurture debate had swung toward the nurture end of the pendulum's travels. Although neither of us studied the issue, Pat and I both embraced the cultural premise of the sixties that any child can be so nurtured as to achieve and embrace the values of the loving family that provides the right kind of environment. These ideals don't conform well to the more complex realities of the twenty-first century, but they established the firm foundation on which we built our family. In retrospect, I believe that our ideals nonetheless provide optimum guidance for the behavior of adoptive parents as long as they understand deep in their hearts that their best efforts can be influential in the development of their children, but not determinative.

Not every couple is well suited for adoption, even in the absence of racial differences. Each child is unique, and even couples who create their own children with their inherited genetic traits can be challenged by the need to accept their children as they are. Adoptive parents know better than to think that they can shape their children to their own images, but this lesson of the mind must enter the heart for adoption to succeed. Even if the adoptive parents can genuinely delight in the discovery of their children's singular identities, they must convey that understanding to their children or face the prospect that the kids will expect of themselves what perhaps cannot be.

Adoption is a challenge not only for the parent and child but for the entire extended family, and especially for grandparents. Attitudes toward adoption are evolving over time, with each generation becoming more accepting of the concept, but even those grandparents who try hard to accept children born outside of the family as their own grandchildren may find it difficult to do so, especially if they grew up in a culture that attached high value to ancestry.

Acceptance by the extended family may be particularly difficult when the adopted child differs in physical appearance from the adopting parents. My advice to any couple contemplating interracial adoption is to discuss the matter if they wish with people experienced in interracial relationships, but not with their parents, who will almost surely advise an easier course. Overruling such well-meaning parental advice can put the adopted child in permanent jeopardy, so if you really want to go forward, be careful whose advice you seek. In our case, Pat and I did not ask anyone for advice, except in some cases our own children.

We understood instinctively that an interracial family must be strong enough to stand alone. We knew that it would be easier for our children if we had a large family with such variety that no one could feel isolated by differences. It seemed obvious to us that our children must be acquainted with the facts of their birth at such an early age that they would accept their adoption without question or anxiety. (We didn't wait for our children's adolescence to communicate the "facts of life," as my mother did, and through a book entitled *The Stork Didn't Bring You!*) We knew that our children were comfortable with adoption when one of them came home from first grade with the astonishing news that some of their classmates actually lived with the parents who had made them. In early childhood our kids thought of adoption as normal and of racial differences as no more significant than differences in height or weight. Of course, in time they learned that not everyone sees the world this way, but by that time their sense of values was well established.

Americans accept adoption more easily than most of the world's peoples, for quite fundamental reasons. A distinguishing characteristic of the culture of the United States is its emphasis on individual achievement, as opposed to family lineage. This is not true to such a degree in all countries of the Americas or elsewhere in the world, but it is our mantra. We want to be judged for what we do and not where we came from. People from the United States often ask strangers when they first meet socially, "What do you do?" We think it's impolite to ask, "What does your father do?" (I remember vividly my raw feelings when a "buddy" of mine asked me this question in front of a girl we were both trying to impress, adding pointedly, "still tending bar?")

Because Americans from the United States are conditioned to evaluate people apart from their ancestry, and because we have always been a mobile population, from the settlers moving west to the young professionals following their work opportunities, we are generally more independent of family traditions than people from other countries. This can be a good trait or not, but it does contribute to the acceptance of adoption in general and interracial adoption in particular.

When people who look like me wonder about cultural opposition to interracial adoption, the concern usually focuses on what might be encountered in white families or the white community. Such arrogance is quickly dispelled when one encounters hostile responses in the "other" community, whether Native American, black, Asian, or whatever population an adopting white family is seen to be "raiding." Upon reflection, this reaction should not be surprising.

Native American grandmothers have stark memories of the time not so long ago when white men literally tore Indian children from their mothers' arms to transport them across the country to boarding schools, attempting (they believed) to acclimate them to "civilization." How does a Native American grandmother feel today when a white family wants to adopt her grandchildren?

Being black in America is not just about skin color or other evidence of African heritage. As visiting students from Africa or the Caribbean have made clear to me, a distinctive African American culture has emerged from the generations of slavery and Jim Crow policies in the United States, and that culture (like any culture) has a stubborn pride. When a white family adopts what Americans call a black child (often actually biracial), that child has been taken from one culture and transferred to another. Tormented by shadowy memories of slave children sold away or transported to the "big house" of the slave owner who fathered the child, black folks in America can feel real distress when a rich, white family adopts a poor, black child.

Probably the first nonwhite children to gain acceptance as adopted children in America were children from Japan or another Asian country in which American soldiers fought wars and left their mixed-race offspring behind. Resentment is an inevitable consequence.

So this has not been easy, this evolution of acceptance of adoption, and especially of interracial adoption. It is, however, getting much easier, in part because of cultural changes quite apart from adoption. Attitudes about race are changing fast, and that will change the entire calculus of adoption.

## Lora

Pat and I first saw Lora as an infant only eight hours after her birth on January 24, 1963, and three days later we took her home with us as our first child for adoption. We were living in married student housing at Stanford Village and I still had a year or so to go for my doctorate, but we were ready to be parents after seven years of marriage, both twenty-six years old.

～ *Pat with baby Lora (1963). (Family photo.)*

Such early placement was possible because California laws permitted the direct transfer of a child from birth mother to adopting parents without an intervening adoption agency. With doctors and lawyers as intermediaries, Pat and I responded to the needs of a pregnant girl who could not raise her baby herself but wanted a good family for that child. Pat's mother had no reservations about adoption; she was the one who made us aware of this child.

Six months would go by before we could receive the necessary home visits in our apartment and secure the approval of government agencies and the courts, but when we left the hospital with Lora she was, in our hearts and minds, our child.

When we took Lora a few weeks after her birth to Stanford Hospital for a routine physical exam, we were stunned by the discovery that she had a life-threatening hole between two chambers of her heart.

"Take her back," insisted her doctor. "She is too small now for surgical intervention and she will not live long enough to become viable for surgery."

Pat stood her ground, but I literally sank to the floor. We did not surrender our child. The young woman who advised us so firmly to "return" the infant had no concept of what it meant to us to accept a baby for adoption. A birth child could not have been more our own from her first breath. Adopting a child is for us not some kind of tentative, trial arrangement to be reevaluated when more information is available. Accepting a child for adoption is for us a lifelong commitment, even before the authorization of the courts.

We were ecstatic to have Lora, by our lights the most beautiful baby in the world. With just the slightest encouragement, Pat would show Lora's baby pictures to any passing stranger, eager to share her excitement about being a mother to such a special child. We put away in some dark place the fear that Lora's heart would not enable her to thrive, and we were right to do so.

For the next dozen years, Lora was under the watchful eyes of a series of pediatric cardiologists in hospitals from Stanford to UCLA to Columbia University, each year with everyone marveling at the continued healing of the wound in her heart (which was felt in our hearts as well). By the time she entered high school the hole in her heart had closed naturally and she was cleared for the track team. Lora has no discernible heart problem as an adult, now in her mid-forties.

I will have more to say about Lora as this story unfolds, but I want to jump ahead now briefly to her freshman year in college at age eighteen. She was then at Ithaca College in Ithaca, New York, and the family home was in Bethlehem, Pennsylvania, a day's drive away. We moved her to Ithaca in September and planned to bring her home in November for the Thanksgiving Holidays.

While Lora was gone, Pat and I received a letter from a woman named Carol McFeron Signet, a stranger to us. We were not strangers to her, however. When she signed the release papers as Lora's birth mother more than eighteen years earlier, she had seen my name on those papers and discovered that I was then a Stanford student. For all those years she had quietly followed me through the Stanford Alumni Association as my faculty career took me from Stanford to UCLA to Columbia to Lehigh University in Bethlehem, Pennsylvania.

Carol wrote a beautiful letter to us as Lora's parents, asking our permission to contact Lora. Of course we agreed, but not without painful reflection. We asked Carol to wait until Thanksgiving so we could deliver her letter to Lora personally. She agreed to wait.

Among the many challenges of adoption is the need to be prepared to respond in a healthy way if a birth parent (or both) reappears in the life of your child, whether from the child's initiative or that of the biological parent. Even if you are very secure in the love of your child, this moment can be unsettling for everyone involved.

Lora's way of handling this new presence in her life was to establish contact gradually, relying upon letters and audiotapes for several years before she found the opportunity to visit Carol on the West Coast in the presence of Pat's mother, who had first become aware of Carol's need to find adoptive parents for her unborn child. In part because our daughter and her birth mother handled it so well, Carol's arrival has added a new and welcome dimension to our expanded sense of family and provided a special presence for Lora. Carol has become Pat's friend and mine as well. When she visited Lora later in Pennsylvania, Carol stayed in our guest bedroom rather than make camp in Lora's smaller house.

With Carol's help, we tracked down Lora's birth father a few years later. I flew with Lora from Pennsylvania to a Likins family wedding in California, rendezvoused with Bob Barker and his wife over breakfast in Palo Alto, and flew back to Pennsylvania alone, leaving my daughter with the stranger who is biologically her father. Lora handled this adventure magnificently and expanded our family once again.

Without pretending to any scientific conclusions, we enjoyed adding evidence to the nature-versus-nurture debate by observing signs of features that Lora shared with one or the other of her biological parents. Although physical similarities were not striking, we all noted commonalities of personality between Lora and her birth father, who never saw her until she was more than twenty years old. Bob Barker was by profession a toxicologist but by avocation an airplane pilot and small-boat captain with a sense of adventure that had drawn him to live with his wife and daughter for several years on the South Pacific island of Palau. Lora's adventures were not so dramatic, but she earned her pilot's license and traveled the world at every opportunity. She tried bungee jumping only once, but that makes one more time than anyone else in our family. Is it possible that Lora Likins and Bob Barker share an "adventure gene"?

When we decided to adopt Lora, we were on what appeared to be very safe ground. Her birth parents were not so different from Pat and me at an earlier stage of our lives when we were struggling students, but our paths kept us together and theirs did not, with a baby accelerating their breakup.

The drama of Lora's medical vulnerability was a shocking reminder that there are no guarantees in childbirth. There can be no expectations of guarantees in adoption, either. Only in retrospect did we realize that our precious infant would have been relegated to the "practically unadoptable" category by the social services bureaucracy had she been placed in the care of a public adoption agency. Lora was the first "practically unadoptable" child we adopted into the Likins family. By the archaic standards of the time, there would be five more. Any child who by virtue of medical infirmity, age, or race offered little prospect of being matched with very selective adoptive parents was for all practical purposes unadoptable.

## Paul

Happy with our decision to begin our family even before I finished graduate school and eager to make up for the years without children, we soon identified another pregnant young woman who sought an adoptive family for the baby she could not raise herself. Pat's dearest friend from high school, Cookie Barrientos, had finished nursing school, which she had begun with Pat, and in her role as a nurse she found the woman we had been seeking. With one of my old high school friends, Bob Newton, as our lawyer, we made the necessary arrangements and brought our son Paul home with us just a few days after his birth on November 10, 1964. We had by that time moved to Los Angeles, where I had just begun a new faculty job at UCLA.

The circumstances with Paul were more complex than with Lora. Paul's birth mother was a Mexican American woman married to an absent husband, also Hispanic. Paul's birth father was an American of Germanic heritage. After they released their child for adoption and we had brought our new baby home, they apparently had second thoughts, both about their own continuing relationship and about the child they had conceived together. We were blissfully unaware of these developments, which were of great concern to Bob Newton as our lawyer. In time the crisis passed and Bob could tell us how close we came to losing our son. We nearly lost Paul, just as we had nearly lost Lora. There are advantages in the earliest possible placement of an infant for adoption, but there are risks as well.

It's difficult to imagine now, in the twenty-first century, the burdens placed on children of mixed heritage needing placement for adoption fifty years ago. Agencies sought the closest possible match of parents and child and most adopting parents did too, acting as though the fact of adoption could be a family secret that need never be revealed. These obstacles to adoption placement began to ease in the mid-sixties, but the practice of placing children with adopting parents of matched heritage and other matching characteristics (such as religion) was the norm before the social revolution in America we experienced beginning in the 1960s. The gradual liberalization of adoption protocols in that era made our family possible through adoptions subsequent to Lora and Paul, but because these first two were private placements we escaped these constraints. As the birth child of a Mexican American woman, Paul would not likely have been placed in the Likins family by any public adoption agency of that era. He might not have been placed at all.

In the twenty-first century not every American can appreciate the burdens of prejudice borne by Mexican Americans fifty years ago. In some parts of the United States, marriage between "whites" and "Mexicans" was then forbidden by law, as it was for whites and "Negroes" or whites and people of Asian descent. Only in 1967 did the U.S. Supreme Court overturn all state laws that prohibited interracial marriage. Institutionalized prejudice of this kind has an insidious effect on the victims, who often internalize the bias.

In my high school years, classmates sometimes were pressured to identify themselves in ways designed to disguise their heritage. If the boy Pat dated over her daddy's objections was Cuban, as rumored, he never said so publicly. Just as Pat's friend Cookie Barrientos was advised by her mother to conceal her Filipino heritage by claiming to be Spanish, a pretty, dark-eyed girl whom I dated in high school described herself as "Spanish," not "Mexican." I didn't care, but apparently she did.

~ *Paul and Lora (1968). (Family photos by James Hansen.)*

Our son Paul carries his Mexican American heritage proudly, but his birth mother could not have escaped the damage routinely inflicted on Mexican Americans during her childhood.

Pat and I really didn't much care about any of this at the time. We had Paul as well as Lora, both beautiful children, and that's all we cared about. We believed that Lora's heart problem would somehow be manageable and Paul's heritage was inconsequential. He was such a good-natured child that he slept through the night before he was a week old. Paul was a very lovable baby and he became a very handsome, intelligent, and loving little boy. Nothing else mattered.

As I found my way through the ranks of the UCLA engineering faculty and Pat made a comfortable home for the four of us in our first real house in the San Fernando Valley, we seemed to be settling down to the family life that we had so long deferred.

Then Pat discovered baby Krista being interviewed on our television screen, and our world changed forever.

# 3

# More Kids

## Krista

Pat was at home one afternoon in 1968, sick with the measles and watching a movie on television. The host of the show, Ben Hunter, dedicated fifteen minutes between films to "Adoption Interviews," introducing to his audience children then thought to be "unadoptable" because of race, age, or infirmity. Ben Hunter was breaking through the barriers of prejudice that excluded entire categories of children from adoption, believing that these barriers would fall if potential parents could see these children as individuals. He hoped that somewhere in his television audience each one of his vulnerable guests would touch someone's heart.

Pat fell in love at first sight with a four-month-old African American baby girl (actually of mixed black/white lineage). When Pat told me about this child, she may as well have said, "I'm pregnant." Another child was about to join our family.

I don't remember any discussion in our household about the concept of interracial adoption. A specific, adorable child had flashed across Pat's television screen and entered my wife's heart, not just for the moment but permanently. That child had been born to a white woman of Polish and Italian extraction and conceived by an absent biological father described as a black man who, although dark in color, had French as well as African forebears. By the social conventions of our society, she was therefore a black child. This put her in a category that the National Association of Black Social Workers declared in 1972 to be appropriate for adoption only by black parents (although Pat and I were blissfully ignorant of any such opposition when we adopted Krista in 1968). I do wonder sometimes if the people subscribing to such constraints understood the odds against finding black parents for every black child in need of a family. These issues of race were interesting background details for us, far less important than the fact that she was a beautiful baby with an expressive, animated look in her sparkling, dark eyes. I knew my wife pretty well by that time, and it didn't occur to me to wonder at this magical event any more than I would question any other manifestation of Pat's loving spirit. If there were to be obstacles to our adoption of a black child, we would find a way to overcome them. We had no doubts, no hesitation.

The Los Angeles County Department of Adoptions may have harbored doubts, or maybe the social workers were just professionally cautious. Almost three months dragged by before we were permitted to claim our child. Even then the social workers seemed apprehensive as they engaged us in small talk while our baby cried in the adjoining room. They didn't know my wife well enough to realize that she would be undaunted by any baby's wrinkled face or crying eyes. When Pat insisted on going to our child, she held her close and wiped away the tears, soothing her fears and bonding with her forever. Krista quieted down quickly and remained content as long as she was in her new mother's arms. We brought our new daughter home with us that day. She was seven months old, born on January 24, 1968, exactly five years to the day after Lora's birth.

The next day, and every day thereafter for what seemed like weeks, Krista clung to her new mom desperately and wouldn't let go. I have a clear image in my mind of my wife going about her household chores with this little tyke balanced on her hip, a contented mother fixing meals for her family and caring for Lora and Paul with Krista snugly attached to her body. Our new daughter craved affection and both Pat and I did all we could do to meet her needs. Gradually she calmed down, perhaps sensing after a while that we were not going to abandon her. Krista became a happy baby, full of giggles and smiles, and as a little girl she was easy to please and eager to please others.

We lived at the time in Granada Hills, an easy commute to my job at UCLA. Pat and I had walked the neighborhood knocking on doors for Tom Bradley's mayoral campaign, so we knew that we lived in a neighborhood with very few people of color. (We discovered one black resident, a musician with the familiar name "Bo Diddley.") When we showed up with a black child, our immediate neighbors sent a delegation to our house welcoming our new baby. We accepted their gesture in the positive spirit that was intended, yet we were not unaware of the implications of their belief that such an official visit was necessary.

Krista was a lovely child and she received a lot of attention from strangers as well as friends and family. When Pat and I took the kids

~ Krista (above,
1968; right, 1986).
(Family photos;
1968 by James
Hansen.)

with us to the grocery store, we grew accustomed to friendly overtures from total strangers who stopped to admire our beautiful brown-skinned baby in the shopping cart. But when Pat took Krista to the store without me, she was more likely to receive cold stares from people who presumably imagined a black man in my wife's bedroom. This all gets a little tiresome, and it can lead to seeing racial prejudice when it's not there, but these small experiences helped us realize that we had to accept some responsibility to make America a better place for people of color.

When Krista was ready for preschool a few years later, Pat received a warm welcome when she called a well-regarded school with openings for new children, but she found those doors closed to Krista when Pat brought her to register twenty minutes later. What were we to think?

Although the adoption social workers seemed initially a bit hesitant, they became our friends and champions before the adoption courts. Pat was named the "Adoptive Mother of the Year for Los Angeles County," with accompanying publicity. Our story resonated across the country, and we were interviewed by Terry Drinkwater for a national CBS News broadcast and found ourselves among other families portrayed in a *TV Guide* story about interracial adoption. We were surprised by all the media attention then, and from the perspective of the twenty-first century all this fuss seems particularly unwarranted, but it was big news in 1968 when a white couple adopted a black child.

My wife and I had no experience in the social-work profession and minimal education in sociology. We followed our hearts into territory that experts in human affairs understand in very complex and sometimes controversial ways, dealing with statistical realities that were beyond our field of view. We were dealing confidently with one child and one family, undeterred by what might then have been discouraging scholarship about whole categories of people.

Much later in life I read informative studies of the multiracial experience and interracial adoption, but that became the basis for reflection, not a guide to action. (See *The Multiracial Child* by Alvin Lewis for a thoughtful and well-referenced example.) Maybe we were not intimidated because we didn't understand the obstacles that lay ahead.

We were not trying to make news or to change the world. We were simply creating a beautiful family and doing it our way, ignoring the biases of our society. We were not oblivious to the external pressures, however, or unconcerned about the future effects on our daughter. We did not want Krista to grow up as some kind of anomaly in a white family in a white world, so we told the social workers in the L.A. County Department of Adoptions that we wanted another black child, this time a boy. They knew us by this time, and before long they delivered what we needed.

## John

Johnny was a totally different experience. He was born on October 5, 1968, and was about eight months old when he joined our family, just a month older than Krista was when she came to us. Like Krista, he was born to a white woman (described as Irish) and conceived by a black man (described as "light skinned"). In contrast to Krista, John seemed rather somber and unresponsive; we wondered if his months in foster care were lacking in human engagement. Even as an infant he was full of surprises, however, so we could only guess about his earliest formative experiences. In his bath he would lie on his back and submerge his head with eyes wide open, obviously comfortable underwater. Did his foster family have a pool? Much later, as a toddler, John walked into the San Lorenzo River in Paradise Park with everyone watching carefully, and when the water reached his mouth he just kept walking until it was over his head; he then turned around and walked back to the shore, breathing easily.

Johnny was an agile baby, so he was able to climb out of his crib quite early. We had obtained a little transitional bed, only six inches above the floor, so first Lora, then Paul, and then Krista could sleep there when they grew out of their cribs and not be injured falling out of bed. On the very first evening when John was assigned to his new bed, Pat and I by chance had guests for dinner. When Johnny climbed out of that little bed and toddled into the dining room, I cheerfully picked him up and returned him to his bed, happy to demonstrate my fatherly patience. In his stubborn determination to join the family in the dining room he came back twenty-five times, which I counted for the benefit of our guests as I picked him up and returned him to his bed, perhaps with a little pat on his bottom to encourage him to get the idea that he was to stay put. Laughing, I said to our guests, "Tonight Johnny got up twenty-five times, but tomorrow it will be ten times and soon he will learn to stay in bed when told to do so."

This story is notable only because on the second night John was returned to his bed forty times. On the third night he was finally returned to his crib!

John was a very determined individual from early childhood, extremely persistent and strong-willed. These strengths served him very well when he became a serious athlete, but the same qualities made him a great and continuing challenge for his parents.

The solemn look we noted initially in John as an infant soon vanished, replaced by an irrepressible smile and an impish look that signaled his limitless potential for mischief. He loved to hide in the house from his mother, laughing joyfully when she finally found him. This sounds like good family fun, but Pat was concerned when she found him one day on an inaccessible top shelf of a closet, and she was absolutely alarmed when she found him another day inside the clothes dryer with the door just barely ajar.

⌁ *John (above,*
*1979; right, 1981).*
*(Family photos.)*

   Johnny was a marvel and a great joy in our family, which seemed with his arrival to be whole and complete. Finally Pat and I had the four children we needed, and life was good.

   We learned to accept the curiosity of strangers. When representatives of a German magazine asked to visit the house for a photo story for German readers, permission was granted. In creating our personal family we were perceived as making a public statement. We did not seek public attention, but we were not backing away from the declaration of fundamental values implied by our family.

## Prejudice

Like many poor kids, I grew up with very negative feelings about rich people, although I had known very few beyond the seemingly wealthy golfers for whom I caddied at Pasatiempo Country Club. I didn't think of my attitude as class prejudice, but that's what it was.

At Stanford, Pat and I found real friends among the brothers in the Delt House. On a trip to Los Angeles (my first) for the UCLA football game (UCLA 72, Stanford 0), we attended a reception at the home of Tony Thompson, a fraternity brother we both regarded with respect and affection. Only when we entered his home in Beverly Hills did we realize that Tony had to be very rich.

Nothing shatters prejudice like a single exception to a biased rule. Tony never knew how important he was to nullifying the class prejudice that I carried from childhood.

Even as a young adult, however, I continued to harbor a lingering bias toward a class of people totally unknown to me: corporate executives, the rich men who ran America's most powerful business organizations. Not until I moved from my UCLA faculty job to Columbia as dean of engineering at age forty did I actually begin to meet these aliens, and I had another epiphany. Bob Lilley, then the president of AT&T, was the head of the college alumni association when I arrived at Columbia in 1976, and Pat and I found Bob and his wife, Helen, to be wonderful people, warm and friendly to us and utterly unpretentious. I had to abandon another prejudice in the face of contrary evidence.

Of course, I later met many more corporate executives in New York and beyond, finally concluding that they are just as varied in their human qualities as professors or truck drivers.

Although Pat and I both grew up in families whose forebears had migrated from regions of America where overt racial prejudice was pervasive, those biases never took root in our hearts as we grew up in California. As a small child I was simply oblivious to these matters, not in any sense enlightened. My grandfather owned a mongrel cat named "Dago" and a black dog called "Nigger," epithets that I accepted without question. (Pat's family had a beloved black cat also called "Nigger," so my family's insensitivity was not unique.)

Children's values are based initially on those of the adults in their families, but gradually they develop a sense of right and wrong on a broader foundation. In the sixth grade I recall feeling mortified when my teacher released the class for recess with the common admonition, "Last one out's a nigger baby!" Belatedly recognizing the one black child in our class, she then said, "Oh! I'm sorry, Jean." I wanted to crawl under my desk.

When I first met Pat in 1950 she was barely fourteen, still trying to internalize the secret of her discovery that her "daddy" was not her birth father and putting some distance between herself and the Jolley clan culture. That family was very close-knit, with the patriarch and two of his sons living on a single tract of land in two small houses and a house trailer. (When I later became acquainted with the Snopes family in William Faulkner's novels, I saw similarities with the Jolley clan, including a character in each family named "Panic" and born on the day of an infamous Wall Street panic.)

Pat's speech showed none of the "southern accent" that typified the Jolleys. She was breaking with their Southern Baptist Church affiliations and attending Catholic mass with her friends. She was actively challenging the racial biases of her family culture, risking her stepfather's anger by chiding him for the racial slurs that peppered his speech. She was throwing out the baggage of her childhood, and prejudice of any kind went out the window. Pat had the quiet support of her mother, who loved everyone, but Juanita was in no position to challenge her husband's family. Pat had no fear.

When Pat and I adopted Krista in 1968, we gave no warning to our parents (or anyone else). When presented with our new daughter, the Jolley family was sorely tested. I'm told that Pat's Uncle Calvin, with whom I had developed a fine relationship when we worked together on road jobs for the family contracting business, declared that Pat and I were no longer welcome in his home with our black child. Pat's daddy had met our darling daughter and been captivated by this striking exception to his biased rules. He loved little kids generally and he loved his daughter Pat dearly, despite his abuses in her childhood. To his great credit he stood by Krista and Pat against his brother, as the family story goes, telling him that if Pat couldn't pass the threshold of his home, then neither would he. B. C. Jolley became Krista's best defender in the Jolley family. His younger brother Calvin was a good man even then, but he had difficulty transcending the prejudices embedded in his family culture. In time, Calvin's family and ours became close again, but that was an evolving process.

The message in this little story is the same as the lesson of my experience with Tony Thompson or Bob Lilley. It is very difficult to sustain prejudice against a group of people if you find one individual who proves to be an exception to your bias.

My father was equally virulent in his racial bias, as I recall most clearly from his language (shouting vulgarities out the car window at any "Jap" or "Nigger" who crossed his path in some negative way). Unfortunately, he never got to know my children, so his biases were never tested in this way.

My sister Katy does recall our father's discomfort when she told him that Pat and I had adopted two more children for a total of six (as discussed in the next chapter). Still unhappy that we had adopted Krista and John, both black, he growled, "I hope they're palefaces."

Katy couldn't resist a grin as she responded, "No, as a matter of fact they are American Indians."

On a more serious note, Bill Likins is reported to have said after the assassination of Martin Luther King Jr., "He got what he deserved." How can anyone even think such thoughts without poisoning his soul?

Religious prejudice was also imbedded in my family culture, but only vaguely so. I certainly knew as a child that we were Protestants and that Catholics were enslaved by mysticism and dogma, but I didn't know any Catholics and I couldn't imagine what that meant. In the fourth grade we chanted "cat-lickers" at the children attending a local Catholic school, and once our verbal war turned to blows on the sidewalk between our schools, but those childhood biases soon faded.

Anti-Semitism was certainly prevalent in America in the 1950s, but hostile feelings toward Jews never penetrated the minds of most kids in Santa Cruz, California. Only in retrospect did I realize that prominent members of the community and the Santa Cruz High School student body were Jewish, including one of my predecessors as student body president.

As I look back upon the days of my youth, I am embarrassed by my lack of awareness of prejudice in its many forms. As a straight, white, Christian male I was a member of a privileged minority and I didn't even think about it. I was so focused on my opportunities when I graduated from college in 1957 that I didn't pause to consider the fact that those opportunities were largely denied to women, gays, and people of color or non-Christian religions. We often hear about the 1950s as a golden age in America, but it was golden only for people like me. While I did not actively share in the prejudices of this era, as a youngster I was not very sensitive to the consequences for most of my fellow citizens. Learning to be prejudiced is easy, but overcoming denial to learn about prejudice is very hard.

I have struggled for my entire adult life to understand the pervasiveness of prejudice, even in the hearts and minds of people who otherwise seem honorable. Where does this come from? Clearly this is learned behavior, not somehow inborn, but it seems to be so easy to learn and so hard to forget. Why is this so?

Prejudices based on race, religion, gender, and sexual orientation have scarred the history of the United States, but at least these feelings and associated behavior are generally contrary to cultural norms in our country today, and in some cases illegal, whereas in other countries similar prejudices are not even understood to be social evils.

What is prejudice, anyway, and why does it die so hard?

In the context of human relationships we understand prejudice to be the prejudgment of an individual on the basis of a category to which he or she belongs. Such prejudgment can cause great injustice and social discord, but this behavior nonetheless persists despite growing awareness of its consequences. We might better understand this persistence and do a better job of minimizing prejudice if we try to think rationally about the mental process we define as prejudicial thinking.

Basically there are two different reasons for the persistence of prejudice in human relationships: (1) Prejudice enables one individual to feel superior to another despite solid evidence to the contrary. (2) Prejudice offers an efficient means for individuals to make judgments about others by providing a single indicator in place of a complex body of knowledge about those other individuals.

Prejudice in the first category is a sickness with no cure, but it can never become explicitly acceptable in society. Behavior based on this kind of prejudice can be outlawed with consequences.

Prejudice based on the second rationale is not inherently wrong; there may indeed be single characteristics that override all other considerations in making judgments about the qualifications of individuals. We might not object to a rule that disqualifies a convicted pedophile from obtaining an elementary education certificate, even as we recognize that a prejudgment is implied. Because this kind of prejudicial behavior is not always unacceptable, it is easy for people who carry a specific prejudice to persuade themselves that their prejudgment is functionally justifiable. As a society, therefore, we must make distinctions between justifiable and unjustifiable prejudice. This is a much tougher task, and it will take a long time to get it right.

If an NBA scout refuses to look at collegiate basketball players under six feet tall, he is displaying prejudice against short people and may create injustice, but few among us would judge him harshly. If he refuses to look at Puerto Rican athletes or Chinese athletes, we condemn him for racial prejudice. This distinction is real, but the scout may see them as equivalent.

How can we most effectively combat this second and more subtle form of prejudice? The answer, I think, is by counterexample, by identifying one individual who is a clear exception to the biased rule. We cannot hope to persuade the NBA scout that it is morally wrong to exclude Chinese players from his field of potential basketball recruits, but we can introduce Yao Ming as proof of his faulty prejudgment.

Tony Thompson and Bob Lilley played this role in dispelling my prejudice against rich, powerful people. Our daughter Krista did the same for B. C. Jolley. If we start looking for individual African Americans who have provided undeniable evidence of the falsity of the stereotype that has plagued black Americans since the founding of our country, we can quickly assemble a very long list of people whose character and public acclaim have done more to dispel racial prejudice than all the antidiscrimination laws on the books. Where would America be today without such famous, mainstream, contemporary black citizens as Jackie Robinson, Arthur Ashe, Michael Jordan, Oprah Winfrey, Bill Cosby, Harry Belafonte, Sidney Poitier, Morgan Freeman, Denzel Washington, Halle Berry, Martin Luther King Jr., Maya Angelou, Toni Morrison, Colin Powell, Condoleezza Rice, and both Barack and Michelle Obama? (Starting such a recitation is risky . . . where does it end?) It is very difficult to sustain prejudice against black people while admiring many of these individuals as exceptions to the biased rule, even as we acknowledge that they share flaws common to us all.

As a general proposition, then, the best way to eliminate prejudice deemed rational by its host is by counterexample, by demonstrating an exception to the biased rule. The best way to eliminate irrational prejudice is to get different kinds of people together in positive ways so they can discover the exceptions to their biased rules, creating cracks in the edifice of their prejudice that will ultimately bring it down. Unless human beings are exposed to good people who are different from themselves in visible ways, they will naturally be disposed to regard such "others" with suspicion and distrust.

As we have learned in our household, differences in race within the family are simply forgotten as we interact with each other over the years. Of course we know that different ones among us have different skin tones and different facial features, but we also vary in height, weight, and age. More importantly, we vary in personality, temperament, and aptitude for different activities. We are all individuals, after all, and we don't make generalizations about the browner ones any more than we make generalizations about the shorter ones.

As a society, we can't wait for the prevalence of interracial families to create new attitudes about race; we need other pathways to this goal.

Athletic teams are excellent environments for the destruction of racial prejudice. Coaches recruit for the kind of athletic talent and personal strength required for success, and no race has a monopoly on these attributes. The bonds among teammates are based on more fundamental qualities than race, which soon becomes irrelevant.

Experience in military combat can also demonstrate the irrelevance of race. Racial tensions in the military often surface during training, but a certain solidarity is developed simply by surviving rigorous training together, and that bond of shared experience often turns to steel in combat. When you can count on your buddy to watch your back, you don't much care what color he is.

Assembling a diverse student body to share a college or university experience is an excellent way to break down inherited prejudice on a large scale. Even a rather conservative U.S. Supreme Court has recognized racial diversity as a "compelling need" of American institutions of higher education, largely for this reason. The Court's 2003 rulings in two cases stemming from the admissions practices at the University of Michigan combine to illustrate the subtle complexities of current law. It is permissible to consider race among other factors in making admissions decisions, but race alone cannot be determinative of admission. The law therefore forbids the adoption of racial quotas in admissions but permits the recognition of race as a surrogate for evidence that a candidate has demonstrated strength of character in overcoming obstacles to academic achievement (just as such obstacles are implied by poverty or a dysfunctional family).

Associate Justice Sandra Day O'Connor, in writing for the majority, expressed the hope and even the belief that American society would evolve over the following twenty-five years in such a way that consideration of race in college and university admissions would no longer be appropriate. In my opinion, this will happen only if we manage in that time to blur the sharp lines that now separate sociologically defined racial categories by recognizing the continuum of humanity that better describes biological reality.

Although it is often said that "you can't legislate morality," it is undeniably true that legal sanctions do modify human behavior and thereby alter the societal norms that influence the moral standards of future generations. In America, the long struggle for civil rights has been advanced immeasurably by all branches of the federal government: executive, legislative, and judicial. Human behavior has been dramatically changed, and new generations have formed their basic value systems in a different social context than their parents knew. Without diminishing or disrespecting these monumental achievements, I would argue that the final steps on this journey must be taken by individual human beings, their families, and social organizations. When we make laws about race we necessarily emphasize the boundaries that separate racial categories. Only when we rise above the need for legislated behavior can we make these boundaries as blurry sociologically as they are blurry biologically, recognizing the human continuum without disrespecting the human variety that populates our country.

The most powerful force in combating racial prejudice, however, is simple human biology, not the law, politics, religion, or sociology. When diverse populations are brought together in continual contact, as they are in school or work or neighborhood living, young people will fall in love without regard to any social boundaries established by the larger society. Babies will be born of unions across boundaries, blurring the lines of separation. The practice of subdividing populations into artificial social categories we call race will become increasingly difficult and those classification decisions will become more arbitrary. American society will continue to be highly diverse, but the distribution will be better described as a continuum over a multidimensional spectrum, rather than as a small list of racial categories. Biology conquers all.

## Family Life

Pat and I moved to Los Angeles in the summer of 1964 for my UCLA job, bringing with us one child, Lora, but soon adding another, Paul. We lived in apartments for that first year and rented a home in the San Fernando Valley for the second year, happily making our way with two children, working hard to establish some security in my new job. In 1966 we moved to Granada Hills into a house we leased with an option to buy, as we certainly had no money for a down payment. A year later we bought the house, assuming responsibility for our first home mortgage. We were a young faculty couple with two kids, beginning what might have become a rather conventional life in Los Angeles.

Then Pat discovered Krista on television in 1968, as described above, and our world changed forever. John joined the family within a year of Krista's arrival, contributing to many new adventures within the family. Outside our home we experienced at the same time student antiwar and civil rights demonstrations at UCLA and nature's demonstration of an even greater power in the form of the San Fernando earthquake. I'll come back to the family and the UCLA story, but first I must deal with nature.

Growing up in California, both Pat and I had felt the vibrations of many small earthquakes, so we had been lulled into thinking of this act of nature as relatively benign, rather exciting but not at all frightening. We were not prepared for what we experienced in the San Fernando earthquake, which registered 6.3 on the Richter scale. When the ground dropped from beneath our feet at our home in Granada Hills in 1971, just a few miles from the epicenter in San Fernando, we were terrified. I was already up for the morning when the earth turned upside down, but Pat was shaken out of bed by the quake. She forgot for the moment that she had invited Krista into our bed between us to still her fears that night, and Pat raced down the hall to rescue the kids. As I snatched Krista from our bed, caught John, and ran down the hall to the room shared by Lora and Paul I found Pat ahead of me, pulling Lora from her bed. Running toward the exit with Lora in her arms, she was thrown to her back by the force of the quake. We all had to scramble desperately to get out safely, joining our neighbors on the street. The concrete-block walls surrounding our home fell to the ground and the house itself cracked at its foundation. When we were able to reenter the house, we found the refrigerator awry and a large bookcase toppled over. The physical damage was extensive throughout the Los Angeles basin, but for most of us the psychological damage was even greater.

Lives were lost in that earthquake, and innocence was lost for millions of Angelenos. Every aftershock created real fear, and even the rumble of a car in a parking structure was a source of anxiety for me for months thereafter. Our four children slept in our bed with us for several months, and the same phenomenon was playing out all over Los Angeles. Child psychologists were in great demand.

So we survived the San Fernando earthquake and student demonstrations in those early years in Granada Hills, but neither influence was more powerful in its impact on our family than John, who was a force of nature in his own right.

John's first experience riding a bicycle was almost as dramatic as his first experience driving a car. In both cases, he demonstrated as a small child his tendency to watch other people do complicated things and then copy their behavior with remarkable skill.

When Krista and John were respectively four and three, our two older children, Lora and Paul, were given 20-inch bicycles that they quickly learned to ride with Daddy initially at their sides. Krista and John could not sit on the seat of either bicycle and reach the pedals, so they simply watched their older siblings have great fun on their bikes until one day John decided that he would not be denied. John mounted Lora's bike and rode off down the road, pedaling while standing and maintaining his balance. We were flabbergasted, but not alarmed.

When soon thereafter he tried the same stunt with Pat's car, we were definitely alarmed. John climbed into the car on his own, released the parking brake, and pushed the gearshift into neutral, trying to steer the car as it slowly rolled down the slightly sloping driveway. Fortunately a brick flower box stopped his progress before he reached the street. No harm was done except to his mother's nerves.

Living with John was always a great adventure.

# 4

# Still More Kids

## Teresa

Ben Hunter's show was not normal television fare for Pat, but she did watch "Adoption Interviews" one more time. A beautiful ten-year-old Indian girl on the show from the nearby Morongo tribe had lost both parents and was languishing in foster care. Our oldest child, Lora, was then nine, and we knew that adopting a youngster with ten years of unimaginable experience behind her would be more difficult than our prior adoptions, but our hearts went out to this little girl and we wanted to learn more. When we inquired, we discovered a very complicated situation that threatened to engulf this lovely young lady, whose name was Terry Marshela Alto.

We have a photograph of Terry's birth mother in Indian attire, mounted on a pinto pony. She was a beautiful woman then, but when alcohol destroyed her life in her early thirties she left behind at least seven children and a husband who soon thereafter fatally ran his pickup into a tree. Her mother, Terry's Grandma Hyde, released all the children as wards of Riverside County; they were separated and lodged with different foster families. In addition to an older half brother, Terry's siblings included two boys aged twelve and nine, two sisters aged eight and seven, and at least one younger child already placed for adoption when we met this family. (There may have been others released earlier for adoption.) Terry specifically asked that her seven-year-old sister, Florenda Maria Alto (known then as "Jonesy"), be placed with her in a new family.

We had four of our own children to think about, aged nine, eight, four, and three, so the idea of adopting a ten-year-old and a seven-year-old was not to be decided by Pat and me alone; we had to have a family conference. We would be creating a family with six children ranging in age over a span of less than seven years, with the first child no longer the oldest child. Lora and Paul gave their enthusiastic blessings and we felt as their parents that they really did understand the implications of this decision. All four of our children knew that they were adopted, but the older two knew what that meant. They knew that these two new girls needed a family and our kids were ready to share.

When our friends at the L.A. County Department of Adoptions were informed of our desire to add two Indian children to our brood, they proceeded with caution. They arranged for Terry and her little sister to meet the whole Likins family in a park for a supervised visit, so we could meet the girls and decide whether or not we really wanted to do this thing. The social workers didn't seem to understand that for us there could be no trial to test for familial compatibility; our decision was made before we met the girls. We asked ourselves if our four adopted children might imagine that they, too, were subject to banishment if we rejected these two new girls. There was no going back for us if we had trouble at that first meeting in the park; the deal was done.

Happily, that first encounter went well and we soon brought home two more children. By that time only the two older Alto boys were still in foster homes, so we arranged for them to visit with their separated sisters for a weekend in our home. We quietly explored with the social workers the possibility of additional adoptions of Alto children, but were discouraged. The older boy, a handsome young man at twelve, knew that their tribal customs often included growing up in foster homes before returning at eighteen to the reservation, and that was his choice.

We adopted the two girls as Teresa Marshela Likins, born April 16, 1962, and Linda Maria Likins, born June 10, 1965, realizing that we would continue to call the older child Terry and her little sister would have to relinquish "Jonesy" for Linda. This was easy, but other aspects of these adoptions were challenging.

Terry was a truly beautiful little girl, but she was also a healthy, athletic ten-year-old who had grown accustomed to fighting for her share of anything she desired. She seemed to be conditioned to present a tough demeanor and a rough exterior. Terry hoarded food against some imagined future famine. She rejected friendly overtures, presumably in anticipation of being rejected herself. She lied as effortlessly as she told the truth. Terry spoke of her childhood only in terms that had to be fantasies. We did not press for more. We knew that it would take limitless patience, unconditional love, and plenty of time to earn Terry's trust.

Over the years we came to see Teresa's tender and gentle soul beneath the gruff exterior and the verbally aggressive bluster. When she finally

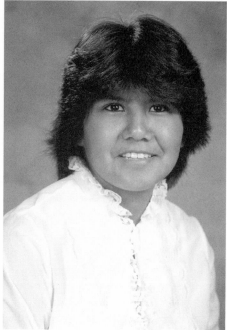

~ *Sisters (left, Teresa, 1977; right, Linda, 1984). (School photos.)*

understood that her new family would never abandon her, she demonstrated a fierce dedication to every member of her adopted family.

## Linda

It was hard for us to keep it in our heads that Terry and Linda were biological sisters. They didn't look that much alike, and they were exact opposites in temperament. While Terry fought for her place in the sun, Linda cowered in fear. Terry was aggressive and Linda was timid. Pat accepted Linda as a neglected child whose development would present a special challenge.

Linda had been classified as "retarded" by people who were educated but not very perceptive; she was retarded only in the literal sense that her development was delayed. She had not had the opportunity to learn what children of her age are expected to learn. She didn't recognize any letter of the alphabet, although she quickly learned to sing the "alphabet song," which recites the letters of the alphabet to music. When she had to pee, she squatted on the lawn, soiling her panties. She was often confused and seemed frightened.

Despite all this, Linda was eager to learn and anxious to please, so Pat found her an apt pupil. Using gold stars on a chart to mark Linda's progress, Pat brought her up to speed very rapidly. She was initially in a class for developmentally disabled children in school, but she grew out of this need and graduated mainstream from high school with no concessions made. We were extremely proud of our daughter.

Linda became a self-sufficient, responsible adult, if sometimes too accommodating of the needs of others for her own good. On her own initiative she qualified by examination as a licensed practical nurse in Pennsylvania, assuring her financial independence.

## Morongo Heritage

Pat and I felt that it was important for both Linda and Teresa to remain connected to their roots, so very early in their time with us we took them back to the Morongo Reservation to visit their grandmother, Agnes Hyde. When we gathered with our children's grandmother and aunt together in their home, Pat whispered to Linda, "You should go hug your grandmother." Linda clung to her new mommy and whispered back, "Which one is my grandmother?" Linda was confused and Terry was characteristically incommunicative, so Pat and I felt very awkward. Mrs. Hyde was, however, very gracious and made us feel welcome. She shared the sad story of her many children, all her sons dead except for the man drinking beer and playing guitar in the backyard. There was little hope in her voice and little promise for what remained of her life. The Likins family left the reservation with her blessings.

Not surprisingly, our Indian children at ages seven and ten had little interest in their heritage and showed no enthusiasm for more visits to the reservation of their early childhood. Pat and I wanted to be prepared to answer any questions about their origins that might come up later in their lives or the lives of their future children, however, so we tried to learn more about the people who inhabited the Morongo Reservation, including Grandma Hyde, whose surname contrasted with Alto, the original last name of our children. We had been intrigued by her observation that no one living at her reservation spoke the language of her childhood, from which we inferred that the people we called Morongo were a composite of unrelated bands of Indians, some of which seemed to have Spanish names. Despite our efforts, we learned very little of the Morongo story in 1972.

Thirty years later, when a grandson in the Indian branch of our family established tribal membership and started to explore the history of his forebears, we began to get some reliable answers. By that time the Morongo had begun to prosper, and with prosperity came pride.

In 2003 the Morongo Cultural Heritage Project produced a celebration and a publication by Ernest Sivo, tribal historian and cultural advisor. *Following a White Eagle: A Brief History of the Morongo Band of Mission Indians* was published in 2003 and revised in 2005. From that source we learn that "the Morongo Indian Reservation is home to individual families representing several different tribes or tribal groups," prominently including "descendants of several Cahuilla and Serrano lineages and clans." The term "Morongo" is historically associated more with a place than with a cultural heritage.

According to the noted reference, the reservation was formally established by presidential executive order as a 640-acre site in 1876. Indian land and water were gradually stripped away to accommodate new settlers until finally in 1911 the tides of fortune turned; the tiny reservation was greatly expanded by federal mandate, eventually encompassing more than 32,000 acres, most of the land rugged and barren but still theirs.

When we visited the cluster of simple homes constituting the Morongo Reservation in 1972, abject poverty was the visible norm. When we returned with our Indian grandchild more than thirty years later, the fortunes of the Morongo had greatly improved. An upscale casino and hotel dominated the skyline as it dominated the Morongo economy. Because casino gambling is illegal in California except on Indian lands, and the Morongo Reservation is perfectly situated on Interstate 10 between Palm Springs and Los Angeles, the opportunity was ripe for transforming the bingo parlor of my Morongo memory into the casino complex and retail outlets that brought wealth to the desperately poor.

I imagine that some entrepreneurial investors were well rewarded by this development, but by policy the tribal wealth has been invested for the general good and well distributed among the membership. Even Teresa and Linda, still formally affiliated with the tribe even in their Pennsylvania residence, have been blessed to receive an unexpected financial boon in their adult lives, and a full scholarship to college has been provided to our Morongo grandson.

Our daughters belong to the traditions of the Morongo Indians, which should be understood in the larger context of the Native Americans who preceded the European Americans on this continent. Most contemporary Americans are familiar with the names of prominent Indian tribes in the Northeast (e.g., the Iroquois), the Southeast (e.g., the Seminole), the Great Plains (e.g., the Sioux), and the Southwest (e.g., the Navajo), but few among us can rattle off the names of Indian tribes who inhabited California before the invasions of the Europeans and their American descendants. Why is this true?

Indians residing in the abundance of California were able to live by hunting and gathering native foods in small family groups or clans as long as they were sufficiently mobile to follow the seasons. In contrast, their cousins in most parts of Arizona, for example, were tied to their croplands and later bound to the range of their livestock. (The same comparisons have been applied to ancient Africa, with Egyptians bound to the Nile to irrigate their crops.) Agricultural societies typically find it necessary to organize work and associated activities more formally than is required by their nomadic contemporaries, and California Indians had less need for tribal structures than, for example, the Hopi or the Navajo. As a result they were less able to resist when white men arrived in the form of well-armed Spanish explorers and their missionary allies, and what little tribal organization they had was soon eclipsed by the invaders.

Vast numbers of California Indians were virtually enslaved as laborers tied to the Spanish missions, whose mission extended well beyond saving souls. Cultures were destroyed and languages were obliterated in the formation of the people we know as "Mission Indians." Sadly, this may be the term that most Americans now know in application to the Indians of California.

When the Spanish empire in North America collapsed into the land we now call Mexico and the boundaries of the United States stretched to the Pacific Ocean, the mission economy collapsed as well. Indians were freed from bondage, but they could not reconstruct the fragile tribal communities of their heritage. They left the missions and resettled as "bands of Mission Indians," like the Morongo.

Does all this history really matter to my children or the generations to follow? I think it does matter. While they cannot allow themselves to wallow in the grief that accompanies the legacy of their forebears, they cannot be allowed to forget the steep climb that has brought their people to a level that permits them to participate in the opportunities of contemporary America.

## California Family

Every one of our six children proved to be a test for us in some individual way, and the addition of the last two was a special challenge because of their ages. However, we never had a moment's regret about any of our decisions to bring these special children into our lives, which were enriched immeasurably. In fact, we were ready to do it again.

When U.S. troops withdrew from Vietnam and Cambodia, hundreds of thousands of allied Vietnamese and Cambodians felt vulnerable to reprisals and desperate to leave their home countries by any means available, often hoping to reach the United States. In the ensuing chaos, with overloaded boats capsizing and communications breaking down, families were separated and many, many refugee children were left without known parents. A humanitarian effort was made to find homes in America for some of these lost children.

Of course Pat and I volunteered to help. The authorities in Los Angeles County, however, denied our application, declaring, "Six is enough!" Indeed, that would have been a different kind of challenge, but we felt that our family could have absorbed such children beautifully, even if we had been obliged to surrender our claim that ours is by birth an "all American family."

Our children became the symbol of our tendency to cross forbidden boundaries in our marriage, but the first such boundary was crossed by joining in marriage as a Catholic and a Protestant. In those days priests were forbidden from conducting such marriages inside the railing that separated the altar from the parishioners, but the retired army chaplain who conducted our wedding ceremony surprised us on our wedding day by ignoring the instructions he had received as a priest. He was my first experience with Catholic priests who stretched the rules a bit, but he was not the last.

After fifteen years of attending mass with my wife and my growing family, I was invited by a young priest named Bill McLaughlin to join him in his work with teenagers, which I agreed to do. Bill knew that I was not a Catholic and could not accept some of the teachings of the Catholic Church, but he also sensed that I was becoming concerned about someday explaining to my children just why I was not a Catholic. Father McLaughlin's vision of the Catholic Church was more inclusive than was perhaps intended by the church hierarchy, and he welcomed me into the fold unconditionally. Every Catholic takes a saint's name

~ *Pat celebrating college graduation (1973) with (left to right) Paul,*
*Lora, John, Krista, Linda, and Teresa. (Family photo.)*

upon baptism, and in recognition of the doubter in the New Testament
he chose Thomas for me.

With the dimensions of our family resolved and my efforts at work
rewarded by promotion to full professor at UCLA, in 1972 Pat and I
bought a home with a pool in Northridge to settle down with our six
kids. We expected to raise our children in Northridge as I pursued a fulfilling career as a professor of engineering, enjoying the combination of
teaching, research, and consulting on spacecraft dynamics that I found
most satisfying.

Pat finished her long-deferred B.A. in English at Cal State Northridge
in 1973, graduating in her cap and gown with six children in tow. In
the following year of graduate study, Pat earned her teaching credential,

realizing in 1974 a goal set in 1958. All six children were enrolled in a nearby parochial school, and Pat got a job there teaching third grade. We were set for life, an established California family.

Pat's sister Barbara and her baby Michelle were welcome additions to our family and a boon to the household during much of our time in Northridge.

Our backyard in Northridge was dominated by a swimming pool that became central to family life. Although Lora, Paul, Krista, and John were already good swimmers, this was a new experience for Terry and Linda. They adapted remarkably rapidly, however, and soon were swimming across the pool underwater, matching the enthusiasm of their new siblings. Linda's success in the pool was particularly gratifying because she needed the praise that comes with doing well. She loved that pool.

I remember well one sunny day when the older four were practicing doing flips on the diving board. They wore T-shirts to take some of the sting out of the occasional belly-flop that made everybody laugh, and after many tries they were all doing a pretty good job of front and back flips.

Krista and John were on the edge of the pool watching the fun, laughing at the flops and cheering the successes. Then John got up on the diving board, ran to the end, and did a perfect flip. He could go forward or backward, without mistakes, having learned by watching his older brother and sisters. John was probably four years old at the time, an amazingly agile little boy, both on the diving board and playing on the lawn.

When Linda and Terry joined our family, John was big enough to ride Paul's little bike comfortably, Krista was able to ride Lora's bike, and the four older kids wanted bicycles for Christmas. In November, Paul's little bike disappeared from the backyard, ostensibly a theft but actually a transfer to a neighbor's garage where I could work on it during spare hours, replacing the seat and handlebars and painting the frame, all so I could present it to John for Christmas without the expense of buying a new bicycle for our youngest child. Krista was to inherit Lora's old bike and she had made it abundantly clear that she wanted an Easy-Bake oven for Christmas, so that was settled. We bought four new ten-speed bicycles for the four older children as Christmas presents (a month's wages for Pat) and gave John the renewed (and unrecognizable) bike that had been Paul's. Everybody was happy except Krista, who was visibly disappointed with her coveted Easy-Bake oven, wishing that she, too, had a new bicycle. She put up such a fuss that the entire family teased her for years about her fickle infatuation with that Easy-Bake oven. Any time she changed her mind about anything at all, she was reminded about that long-ago Christmas.

During the four years in Northridge the children were all thriving individually as well as collectively.

Except for her uncharacteristic pouting over her Easy-Bake oven, Krista was always the sweet, agreeable one, blooming like a beautiful flower. She was our precious "brown sugar," although actually not as dark in color as her Indian sisters.

John established himself very early as the family's chief mischief-maker. We learned to recognize an impish gleam in his eye that signaled his latest misdeed. We learned, too, that he would always tell the truth if we were clever enough to ask the right questions. ("Who let the dog out?" might not elicit the same answer as "Who left the gate open?") John's spirited energy was almost scary; he seemed destined for great achievement or disaster, or both.

Linda was making remarkable progress, opening up as a happy and easygoing child, always trying hard and eager to please.

Teresa (then "Terry") sang the Diana Ross song "Mahogany" on stage in a school show, a lovely girl breaking out of her protective shell and gaining confidence.

Paul's intelligence and verbal facility were more apparent with each passing year; we began to see him as the budding lawyer in the family.

Lora maintained her buoyant spirits and also excelled in school. She always adapted beautifully to our adoption of the brothers and sisters who insisted on sharing the limelight that she had once enjoyed as our only child. Although the pediatric cardiologists could still detect anomalies in her heart, their prognosis was increasingly positive.

Even the family pets were thriving. Little Tuptim, the Siamese cat who preceded all the kids in the family, adjusted well to a growing extended family of children and animals. Bagheera, the big, black panther of an alleycat, joined our family in 1966 and remained among us for almost twenty-four years. Other cats and dogs were with us for shorter lives, but most memorable were three family dogs named Hans, Miska, and Yogi (who was Miska's pup).

Hans was some kind of shepherd mix, by appearance more coyote than dog. Miska, in contrast, was a purebred Norwegian elkhound, the realization of my childhood fantasy. When my brother Tod and I were living in Paradise Park, where pets were forbidden as a threat to wildlife, we substituted long hours with an AKC dog book for the real thing. We chose our favorite breeds from pictures in that book; my choice was the Norwegian elkhound. At age thirty-one I finally acquired a lovely Elkhound bitch we named Miska, and when she was ready to bear a litter we saved a big male we called Yogi. Hans, Miska, and Yogi were important members of our family. Miska died young, but she remains a significant part of the family legend. Decades later Pat gave me as my boon companion in retirement a Norwegian elkhound we called Loki (named after the Norse god of mischief). Pat and I agreed that the weight of my dog on our bed at night could match that of her dogs, but Loki soon outweighed Pat's four precious Shih Tzus and Loki had to retire to her own bed (most of the time). Pat's love for animals, both pets and wildlife, matches her love for children.

In many ways, Pat was the most remarkable member of our family during these years in California. She had always been well organized and resourceful in her management of our household, but as our family increased in both size and complexity she grew into new responsibilities with grace and good humor. As we look back upon these years from our perspective as septuagenarians, Pat and I both wonder where she found the patience and the extraordinary energy required to take proper care of the individual needs of six special children while doing the household cooking and cleaning, taking college courses to finish her degree, and finally teaching a third-grade class. She baked bread as well as cookies, prepared homemade soups and casseroles for the freezer, and found time for needlepoint creations that required real artistry. (Pat put away her oils and canvas when maintaining a home studio became incompatible with motherhood.) Despite all of her responsibilities, Pat was having the best time of her life.

We were settled in Los Angeles and very happy there as just another California family with a full household of kids, cats, and dogs. Why would we ever think of moving?

## UCLA

My work life at UCLA had its own challenges quite apart from the increasingly complicated family that welcomed my return home every evening. This is not the place to describe my efforts to find the right combination of teaching and research for survival in the rigorous UCLA vetting system; it's enough to say that I did learn to swim in these fast waters, earning promotions and tenure on an accelerated schedule. My commitment to my work was intense. Pat carried a heavy load at home, but in those days she rarely showed the strain. Pat really was the super-mom she appeared to be.

My twelve years at UCLA (1964–1976) spanned the period of student protest and demonstrations relating to the war in Vietnam and the battle for civil rights in America, which then focused primarily on African Americans. As an engineering professor, I often learned about police suppression of riotous demonstrations on my campus by watching the evening news on television at home, which made localized conflict on campus seem to be campus-wide. When Governor Ronald Reagan declared an emergency and shut down the UCLA campus, my students and I rebelled by continuing to hold classes, devoting time to social conflict in addition to the technical course material. The university was under siege, but it seemed to me to be under fire from both sides: student demonstrators and governmental forces.

Pat and I realized that in our own way we were making serious commitments to the battle for civil rights for all Americans, and not only with the quiet statement we made by our choice of children. As mentioned previously, we went door-to-door campaigning for the election of Tom Bradley as mayor of Los Angeles, the first black mayor to be elected in that multiracial city. I was the token straight, white male on the UCLA Equal Opportunity and Affirmative Action Committee. Pat and I were not engaged in demonstrations on the streets, but we were becoming increasingly determined to make a positive difference for people of color in our country. We were philosophically in harmony with the protesting students, but we could not condone their tactics. We applauded the determination of these young people to make the world a better place, but we could not support violent demonstrations or even crude behavior. We knew that for many zealous young demonstrators the enthusiasm for noble causes would soon fade, but for us the commitment was permanent.

Although the world-famous University of California had enjoyed enlightened public and political support for decades, in the late sixties it was perceived by many critics as a haven for radicals bent on social revolution. Governor Reagan denied merit raises for all UC professors in a misguided attempt to punish the entire system, and political commentators lambasted the faculty for both political waywardness and indolence. This was a difficult time to be a hard-working professor of engineering in the UC system. I was offended by the damning generalizations.

When a television commentator named Baxter Ward calculated and then broadcast the hourly compensation of the public university faculty, he divided their average annual salary by the number of hours professors typically spent each year in the classroom (six hours a week for nine months at UCLA). The faculty salaries by this measure were of course exorbitant and we were vilified as overpaid, underworked civil servants. I had just completed a weekly accounting of my work activity mandated by the governor and knew that I was working at least sixty-hour weeks, so I was uncharacteristically incensed. I sent Baxter Ward a message: "I don't know how much money you make but I do know that you work thirty minutes a day for five days a week, because I see you in your daily television broadcast. What is your compensation expressed in dollars per hour?" Baxter Ward didn't respond to me, but he did parlay his television popularity into a seat on the L.A. County Board of Supervisors.

My experience at home with an interracial family became intertwined with my role as a UCLA professor in the middle of a national struggle for the civil rights of people of color. Although universities have their share of bigots too, for the most part my colleagues shared my belief in racial equality and the need for greater opportunities for minorities. However, they generally lacked the sense of urgency that seemed to energize the activists whose excesses they deplored. I realized as a parent of minority kids that accepting the plea for patience and gradual reform meant denying my children the opportunities they needed and deserved. Although a white man can never feel the desperate need for urgency that a black man can feel, both white and black fathers of black children are alike in their desire to spare their children from needless harm. I will never be a black man, but at times I know that I shared that man's thoughts and feelings.

Faculty life intersected with my personal life in exciting ways when we were able to combine UCLA work with family play. From an outsider's perspective it may appear that faculty life and family life are most compatible during the months of summer vacation from school, but this ignores the need for concentrated faculty efforts in research whenever classes are not in session. These pressures were financial as well as professional because a UCLA professor with a federal research contract could earn additional compensation for every day actually doing research or communicating its results during the summer months, and we needed that money. So "vacations" were short and almost always combined with a technical conference presentation or similar professional activity.

Nonetheless, all members of our family have great memories of our vacation travels.

We bought a small Layton travel trailer that we could attach to our family's Dodge van for camping trips and packed our family of eight little people into that efficiently designed space for many nights in campgrounds.

When I had a technical paper to present at a conference in Vail, Colorado, we hauled that trailer to Vail from Los Angeles and back, visiting national parks and staying in campsites along the way.

On a rare pure vacation drive south deep into Baja California, we were joined by our dearest friends from our shared student years at Stanford and our shared faculty years at UCLA, Tino and Lynn Mingori, all ten of us packed into the trailer every night in Mexico like sardines in a can. Tino, well over six feet tall, stretched out on the floor of the trailer's narrow aisle. Traveling that way brought us closer together in more ways than one—the Mingoris offered to take in the six Likins kids if Pat and I suffered some disastrous, simultaneous fatalities!

Our children treasured another bonding experience on a camping trip to New Brunswick, Canada, with the Skelton family. Bob Skelton was an excellent Ph.D. student of mine at UCLA and ultimately a distinguished professor at the University of California, San Diego. I was only a couple of years older than Bob, and we shared not only a mutually beneficial academic experience but a personal relationship that included our families. Bob and his wife, Judy, had three boys and a girl, all in the age span of our four girls and two boys. Bob and I had a technical paper accepted for a conference in New Brunswick after he had graduated to a faculty position at Purdue, by which time I was working at Columbia and living in New Jersey. We decided to drive into Canada with our families, camping along the way. We had one tent for the five girls and another tent for the five boys, leaving our travel trailer beds for the four parents. Ten days and ten nights camping with ten kids can be a memorable experience.

The most exciting combination of faculty work and family play was a trip to Europe in 1971, before Terry and Linda joined the family. Pat's mom in Santa Cruz cared for the two littlest ones, Krista and John, who had a rare but special opportunity to bond with their Nana. Lora and Paul, then eight and almost seven, flew with Pat to Hannover, Germany, where I was to rendezvous with them after a week lecturing on flexible spacecraft dynamics in Dubrovnik, Yugoslavia. We had arranged to buy

a Volkswagen camper in Hannover and then to visit European campgrounds as I completed a lecture tour with stops in Munich, Stuttgart,
and Brussels. The itinerary called for my mom to join us in Brussels and
take a side trip to London with Pat and the kids while I lectured for a
week in Brussels. My various jobs on this trip earned enough income to
pay for the trip, which we couldn't afford otherwise.

That was the plan and it worked out perfectly once we connected in
Hannover, but showing up on time to meet Pat's plane in Hannover was
a harrowing experience for me. If she had known beforehand how close
she would come to arriving in a foreign country with no one to greet her
after a very long flight with two little kids, she would have been praying
for a more reliable husband. I almost let her down, and would have done
so if not for a kind stranger who helped me to escape from Yugoslavia.

My flight schedule took me from Dubrovnik to Zagreb, Yugoslavia,
and then to Hannover via Frankfurt, Germany. The flight to Zagreb was
uneventful, but I was not permitted to board the flight to Germany, with
no explanation that I could understand, limited as I was to English. My
airplane took off without me.

As a little man with no language skills in a bustling airport in a Com-
munist dictatorship, I felt very vulnerable. But as so often happens when
people in strange lands need help, an angel came to my rescue. When I
finally got the attention of a woman behind the counter who understood
my dilemma, she explained (in English) that the airline personnel in
Dubrovnik had inadvertently pulled (and retained) the wrong ticket, so
my ticket to Germany was gone but my ticket to Zagreb was still in my
possession. She asked her supervisor if they could put me on the next
flight to Hannover, even with the wrong ticket.

The manager said no, they would wait for the proper ticket to be
delivered on the next flight from Dubrovnik. Then the winds came up
and closed Dubrovnik Airport. My angel told her supervisor that she
would personally pay for my ticket to Hannover if the proper ticket
didn't arrive later from Dubrovnik.

I met Pat and the kids in Hannover on schedule and our trek through
Western Europe was a memorable experience for all of us. My most
powerful memory, however, is the kindness and generosity of the stranger
who made it all possible.

Although I had to overcome some anxieties when I first joined the
UCLA faculty, I soon discovered that this was an ideal job for me. I put
long hours into my teaching, research, and consulting in the aerospace

industry, but I loved the independence and valued the feeling that I was doing something of benefit to society. I paid little attention to the management of the department, the college, or the university, enjoying my own little domain of students and professional colleagues, until a new dean of engineering at UCLA sought me out for a short-term, part-time assignment as assistant dean of engineering. I agreed to serve in the Dean's Office at less than half time for three years, eager to get back to the full-time faculty life that I so enjoyed.

Although I would have denied such ambitions at the time, I do now recall one telltale symptom of my future interest in management. I remember reading to my children a Dr. Seuss book called *If I Ran the Zoo* and thinking quietly to myself that my university would be a very different place if I were in charge. There came a time in my life when in fact I was in charge of a university, and I discovered how difficult it is to change a culture.

My work at UCLA was going extremely well and together Pat and I were managing to maintain a beautiful family life at the same time. We were settled in California, with no intention of leaving our happy home. Then Columbia called with a surprising job offer, and Pat gave her enthusiastic blessing: "Let's pack up the kids, cats, and dogs and move to New York."

# 5

# The Columbia Years

## New York, New York

What do they say in the song? "If I can make it there, I'll make it any-where / It's up to you, New York, New York."

Was this song playing in the back of my head when Columbia's president, Bill McGill, came to UCLA to offer me the job of dean of Columbia's School of Engineering and Applied Science? I was not seeking any new job, although I knew that I had been nominated by a UCLA faculty colleague with Columbia ties. I saw myself then as a UCLA professor on temporary, part-time assignment in the UCLA Dean's Office, a job accepted out of duty, not ambition. I never would have volunteered for a job in New York, which promised to disrupt the lives of my entire California family. My sons and daughters were California kids, accustomed to a free-spirited culture that for the most part welcomed their diversity. What dangers might they face on the East Coast? Would they be okay?

To my surprise, Pat was eager to accept the challenge. Her adventurous spirit was contagious and soon all our kids were ready to say goodbye to their friends and sail into foreign waters. It was a bold move for us to exchange the good life in California for the uncertainties of metropolitan New York, but we realized that our family of eight people was a self-sufficient unit, not reliant upon the approval of others. We knew that we would be okay as long as we had each other.

In my heart of hearts I wanted to go to New York for the same reason that I wanted to enter postseason wrestling tournaments after every successful wrestling season. I needed to test myself, to see if I could swim in the turbulent waters that I knew I would find at Columbia. As soon as I was sure that Pat and the kids were ready for a great adventure, my decision was easy.

And so it has been for my entire professional life. I have never applied for a new job since my first appointment as a UCLA assistant professor.

When invited to step up to a new challenge, I have often declined but three times have been unable to resist, first at Columbia, then Lehigh, and finally Arizona. On each of these occasions, Pat has encouraged me to take the leap of faith, and we have done so together, moving the entire family.

The move from California to New York, however, was the biggest step for all of us, putting in motion all the subsequent changes that came from future opportunities. Life would never be the same for any of us.

Pat and I made every effort to ease the transition for our children, who were fourteen (Teresa), thirteen (Lora), eleven (Paul and Linda), eight (Krista), and seven (John) in the summer of 1976, when we made our move. Pat and I had rendezvoused in New York immediately after she finished her teaching obligations, meeting me on a return trip from Europe, and in four days we had scoured housing opportunities in three states and bought a house in Park Ridge, New Jersey, so we would have a home to move the family into when we arrived by car from California and I would have a tolerable commute into upper Manhattan.

I had more than a month between the end of my UCLA responsibilities and the beginning of my job at Columbia, so we had quality time with the family to bridge the divide between California and New York. We used that time well.

I have always been a responsibility-driven person, unable to banish feelings of unmet responsibilities from the back of my mind even when ostensibly at play. In the summer of 1976, however, I was between jobs and had no obligations but my family. I was quite conscious of the unfamiliar feeling of liberation from duty (only rediscovered thirty years later when I retired).

Pat and I had enjoyed driving across this great country of ours for our year at MIT in 1957–1958. We wanted our kids to have that experience, so we hooked our travel trailer to the family van and meandered with six kids, five cats, and two dogs from campground to campground all across America. We visited Zion and Bryce Canyon national parks in the Southwest, headed north to gaze at Mount Rushmore and experience the South Dakota Badlands, continued east with our trailer whipped by the winds on the freeways south of Chicago, and finally entered New Jersey on its western edge, ultimately reaching our new home in Park Ridge.

We enjoyed this trip so much that two years later we drove that same van and trailer to California and back for a brief vacation, this time stopping at the Grand Canyon.

~ *Together in the travel trailer. Left to right: Linda, Paul, Krista, Pat, Pete, Lora, Teresa, and John. (Family photo.)*

The drive across America has important lessons for every American, but especially for bicoastal residents, who often cannot fathom the vastness of the land between our coastal urban centers. More important than the scenery for the Likins family, however, were the endless hours we shared in close quarters, strengthening the forged bonds that hold our family together.

In the following spring our daughter Lora demonstrated in a composition that she wrote for a competition in school the depth of her understanding of the significance of our family experience. That one-page essay is reproduced below:

### Reflections on the Bicentennial and What the Future Holds

*By Lora Likins, May 1977*

On the fourth of July in 1976, my family and I were in a campground in Wyoming celebrating the 200th birthday of the Revolution and my father's 40th birthday. We were moving from California to New

Jersey with a car load of six all American kids, two dogs and five cats, with two patriotic parents. We felt like the Pilgrims crossing the Atlantic to the New World, or the Western Pioneers going backwards. We were like Revolutionaries set free to face the challenges of a new life in America. Like the Pioneers, Pilgrims and Revolutionaries, we did not know what was in store for us.

We're an unusual American family, with six adopted kids. We are like the Immigrants in America, different races of people with different heritages and customs trying to survive and cooperate in a new land. We have European-Americans, Afro-Americans and American Indians in our family.

We came across the country in a Dodge van pulling a trailor, a modern day covered wagon. We were also like the Trail-Blazers leading the way for other families to follow an example of how not to be so prejudiced against different races. We show we care by trying and making it work. We have our differences, but we still love and care for one another.

Two hundred years ago Americans didn't count the Indians as people, and when the Blacks were brought here they were not counted as people either. But in our family, everybody counts; and in America today, we're all one people.

What does the future of America hold? Nobody knows. But I hope that all people will not be prejudiced against people of different nationalities, religions, backgrounds or whatever their past was. I hope that people will help and care for each other not to hurt, kill or just be mean. I would like to live in peace for the rest of the history of the United States, and even have this peace shared by other countries. Today, in our progress, we are trying to understand different people. Tomorrow we may be able to live in peace with one another. I think that if we push a little harder, we may get to that future sooner than other countries.

Pat and I were proud parents when Lora won her composition contest with this essay. She understood at fourteen, thirty-three years ago, what this book is all about.

As Lora wrote, I celebrated my fortieth birthday in a campground with my family on July 4, 1976, just as Americans everywhere were celebrating the bicentennial of our nation. Never was the birthday I share with the United States of America more meaningful.

## Columbia University

The story of my family runs parallel to the story of my academic career, which is secondary in the present context but primary in its explanation of our position both geographically and professionally.

I was exhilarated by the intellectual atmosphere at Columbia University and challenged by the need to secure for Columbia's engineering dean a position of respect in the very competitive Columbia leadership hierarchy. Columbia's culture was based on relationships much more than I had been accustomed to at UCLA, which was a more rule-based society with established procedures. I enjoyed my role as an innocent young dean from the West finding my way among older and more sophisticated players in the campus political arena.

To a remarkable degree I found the Columbia University I discovered in 1976 still struggling from wounds inflicted during the late 1960s, when student protest over the war in Vietnam melded with community opposition to Columbia's plans for expansion into its black neighborhood to ignite a major conflagration.

The stories of student revolt on college campuses from UC Berkeley to Columbia and in between were polarized and grossly oversimplified in the media and in political circles at the time, with university administrators vilified by angry students as despotic, right-wing reactionaries and simultaneously condemned by opportunistic public officials as weak-kneed, liberal apologists for dangerous revolutionaries. The reality was much more complex and multidimensional.

Research universities are not monolithic, homogeneous enterprises; political opinions within a fine university can be found at all points along the ideological spectrum. Insofar as I might be tempted to generalize, I would characterize the politics of faculty and students by their college affiliation within a university, with engineers inclined to the right and humanists generally disposed toward the left (with important exceptions in every college). These internal differences surfaced in the campus conflict at Columbia, but the popular perception was polarized as a battle with students and faculty on one side and representatives of "the establishment" on the other. Because Columbia alumni generally shared the public perception, many successful alumni felt betrayed by their alma mater, showing their displeasure by withholding their customary gifts and urging their offspring to go elsewhere for their college education. Engineering alumni are also inclined to be politically conservative as a whole, and their anger was directed at their own School of Engineering and Applied Science, whose students and faculty were typically not involved in campus revolts and were on some occasions even protective of the university administration.

The disaffection of Columbia's engineering alumni could be measured by the flow of annual gifts to the school. When I arrived as dean in 1976 these numbers were dangerously low, and it was 1980 before annual gifts to the engineering school matched the levels routinely received in 1968, before the revolt on campus.

I learned more about university politics than I really wanted to know in my four years as dean of engineering at Columbia.

I was as surprised as anyone when, four years after my arrival at Columbia, I was invited by Columbia's new president, Michael Sovern, to become provost of the university, joining in that office a very distinguished member of the Columbia history faculty, Fritz Stern. We must have seemed to many observers to be an odd couple to share the job of provost of the university, but we worked together so well for the next two years that we were generally perceived as one fine provost. President Sovern made a bold move in inviting our elevation to this assignment and it was a good decision. I learned in those years how powerful a partnership can be if egos can be set aside for the good of the organization.

In retrospect, I can look back upon those pivotal years in my professional development with gratitude for the opportunities and pride in my performance. I need to remind myself quite consciously that my six years at Columbia were also a time of enormous significance to my wife and children and to my home life in New Jersey.

## New Jersey Family

The borough of Park Ridge is a small community in the northeast corner of the state, less than an hour's drive across the George Washington Bridge to the Columbia campus on Manhattan's Upper West Side. I drove to work very early every morning in my little 1975 Honda Civic, but I was generally home for evenings and weekends with my family. Six years later, this kind of freedom vanished when in 1982 I became a university president, but by then our children ranged in age from thirteen to twenty and the time demands of parenting were much reduced. I was there for my kids during our New Jersey years despite the increasing demands of my job at Columbia.

Pat couldn't find a teaching job in New Jersey. After a brief stint as office manager for two psychiatrists in the area, Pat became a full-time mom, so she was always there for our kids.

Adolescence is a time of stress for every child, as a sense of self emerges and the need for an independent identity begins to surface. What's true for every adolescent is doubly true for an adopted child. Feelings of nascent rejection and rebellion are compounded by concerns about race and sexual identity. In our family these tensions were all beginning to develop during our six years in New Jersey, but for the most part they stayed beneath the surface. We were a very close family, actively involved in each other's lives. Six kids kept us all very busy as their lives expanded into new activities, ranging from sports to music and theater, and Pat and I enjoyed being stretched in all directions.

With Times Square only an hour's drive away, we wanted to expose our children to theater on Broadway, but the price of eight tickets even then was a huge deterrent. We discovered that every Saturday morning there were half-price tickets centrally available for any Saturday matinees not already sold out. It was not unusual for us to pack the whole family into my two-door Honda Civic hatchback and drive into Manhattan on a Saturday morning, choosing a show on the spot from those available and enjoying whatever surprise awaited us. I'm sure we looked like a bunch of circus clowns as all eight of us piled out of that tiny car, but our Dodge van was more difficult to drive and park in Manhattan so we drove the Honda, just as we did when we took in the sights of Manhattan during the Christmas season. We all have wonderful memories of those excursions into the city, but we made our home in New Jersey.

Pat's theatrical performances in high school were twenty-five years in her past when she was persuaded to take the stage again in the lead role of a community theater production of *You Can't Take It with You*. The cast of Park Ridge High School parents and teachers was so well received that they were encouraged to take the show on the road, but that didn't happen.

Among the children, Paul was most involved in high school theater. I have a vivid memory of Paul onstage with fellow dancers in black hats and white gloves doing the "Steam Heat" number from *Pajama Game*.

All of the kids had piano lessons, but their interests soon faded or migrated to different instruments. Paul's guitar became an important part of his life for many years, culminating in a stint in a professional rock band as a young adult in New York. Lora played her flute throughout

 *New Jersey family at home (1977). Left to right: Paul, John, Teresa, Krista, Linda, and Lora. (Family photo.)*

high school and college. Linda followed Lora into the high school march-ing band with her clarinet. John's choice, not surprisingly, was the drum, which he played for a time in a marching drum and bugle corps. Krista also chose the drum, but her marching band experience was limited to clanging cymbals and was not sustained.

The point in this description of our kids' involvement in music and theater is simply to reflect on our life as a typical American family. The family's involvement in youth sports activities tells a similar story that I will set aside for the moment. We may have seemed a bit unusual on first encounter, but the visible differences were soon forgotten in the normal course of life.

My responsibilities at Columbia did not keep me from scheduling time with my children but did put limits on any significant spontane-ous time commitments. Wise beyond her years, Lora figured out how to engage me as the designated parent for various offbeat adventures. She came to realize that I would commit to almost anything if given enough notice to get it on my calendar, so she planned six months in advance.

I joined Lora and her friends in a rubber raft on the rapids of the Lehigh River, pulling a laughing Lora from the water when she fell overboard. On a canoe trip with the same girls I discovered quiet and lovely waterways that most visitors to New Jersey never imagine. Lora claimed a special place in my heart by reaching for it.

Each of our children will savor different memories of our time in New Jersey, but all will share a memory of the imaginary invention game we played together for years. Any of the kids could start the game at any time by posing for my immediate response the question, "Who invented _____?" They inserted whatever came to mind, such as ice cream or bicycles or pretzels. Always the answer was the same: "Hans the baker man, who lived in a Swiss village with his wife, Miska." (Recall that our family then included two beloved dogs named, by coincidence, Hans and Miska.)

The children knew, of course, that "Hans" would be credited with every invention, but they waited eagerly for my explanation of the story of each new idea. My challenge was to start telling each new invention story before I knew how I could get the tale to end with the remarkable creation the child had named. Before the children grew too old for this silly game, Hans had invented dozens of familiar items and I had spun some fanciful yarns now mostly forgotten.

When Hans was a young baker's apprentice he had the job of delivering fresh bread to the villagers. One day he had in his backpack for a trek up a snowy mountain not only bread but a goatskin containing separate packages of milk, butter, eggs, sugar, and cocoa for a group of mountain climbers at their base camp. Hans slipped on the ice as he neared his destination and tumbled head over heels down the snowy slope, all the way to the bottom. Unhurt but embarrassed, he climbed back up the icy trail to the base camp and discovered in his backpack a goatskin filled with a frozen concoction of milk, butter, eggs, sugar, and cocoa all mixed together. Rather than acknowledge his clumsy fall, Hans presented the climbers with a new gourmet's delight he called "ice cream." And that, boys and girls, is how Hans invented ice cream.

Did you know that the bicycle was invented by Hans as a brilliant insight following an accident involving two unicycles that got all tangled up with each other?

Some of the memories treasured by our kids were not shared with their parents until they felt that the passage of time had made their stories safe. Paul and Teresa laugh about the day they held John upside down out the second-story window of our home, each hanging on to an ankle. Krista remembers John being stuffed by his siblings into a carrier intended for cats. They insist that John deserved such abuse and they are proud of him for keeping his silence.

I could hardly have complained about my children's abuse of their younger brother, remembering how Tod and I had treated our little brother Jimmy. Although Jim remembers being tied up by his older brothers and rolled under the bed, I have suppressed that memory. More unforgettable is the blood Jimmy shed after he straight-armed the half-glass door when Tod and I threw him out of the cabin in Paradise Park. All this, and Jim was much less prone to mischief than his nephew John.

Pat and I find it easy to believe that Johnny drove his brother and sisters to harsh retaliation on occasion; he sometimes stretched our patience as well. John bought a dirt bike with money he had saved from his paper route and he knew that this mini-motorcycle was not legal on public streets. When he violated this prohibition, we locked the dirt bike in a steel shed in the backyard. When we returned home that day the padlock was intact, but the door had been removed from its hinges. John knew he'd be in trouble when he got home that day, but he had clearly decided that the joy of riding his bike was worth the grounding that was sure to follow.

Remembering my own adolescent excesses with alcohol and anger, I would have been surprised if my sons had passed through their transitional teenage years without problems. Initially I was more apprehensive about John, but Paul entered that dangerous age first and caught me unprepared. There was a lot happening in Paul's life that I didn't understand, and his mother's support was often misunderstood as unduly constraining. Paul's grades did not reflect his intellectual capabilities and he didn't seem to care. I worried about Paul and I worried about my inability to connect with him at this critical stage of his development. Pat was better than I, but not good enough to meet Paul's needs.

Teresa, Lora, and Paul graduated from Park Ridge High School before the family moved again in 1982. Teresa made a brief attempt at nursing school before opting for other training for hospital service (which served her well). Lora enrolled at Ithaca College in New York, far enough from home to declare her independence but close enough for a rapid-response visit from her parents when she had emergency surgery for appendicitis. She majored in speech pathology and audiology, a strong major at Ithaca College, exploring her established interest in deaf education. By the time she graduated from Ithaca, Pat and I had moved to Pennsylvania with the three younger children. Paul followed Lora to Ithaca College a year after her arrival there, but he was immediately unhappy and often delinquent, spending long weekends in New York City, where he felt more comfortable. We succumbed to his entreaties and he started his freshman year all over again in Manhattan at the Fashion Institute of Technology, majoring in photography, which for Paul was an established interest. That venture also lasted only one semester and Paul remained in Manhattan an angry dropout.

Paul's story promises to have a happy ending, but the New Jersey chapter in Paul's life was not easy for anyone and was a particularly difficult time for Paul.

## Park Ridge Athletic Club

As a boy I had no opportunity to participate in organized sports until I was a sophomore in high school, when my mother remarried and we moved into town. The sports in which I later excelled, wrestling and lineman's football, were surrogates for combat and not games to play for fun. I wanted my children, all of them, to have the opportunity to play sports for fun.

In the New Jersey borough of Park Ridge, when we arrived in 1976, a wide variety of sports were available for boys and girls under fifteen through the auspices of the Park Ridge Athletic Club (PRAC), an independent organization run by parents and friends of the hundreds of kids involved. Before long, all six of our children were on PRAC teams, playing soccer, football, softball, baseball, and basketball. (Our kids were also learning to swim competitively under auspices apart from PRAC.) Pat and I were naturally drawn into the athletic club, coaching teams and organizing events.

In accordance with the culture of that time and place, the Park Ridge Athletic Club was governed by an all-male board (fathers) complemented by a women's auxiliary (mothers). Pat's organizational skills became so valuable to this board of busy men that they asked Pat to be their secretary. The following year they recognized that she deserved to be president of the board. As president, she dissolved the women's auxiliary and welcomed other women to full membership on the governing board.

Pat made such an impression over her years of volunteer service in Park Ridge that the Democratic Party persuaded her to run for town council. She effectively withdrew from the race when we moved in 1982 to Pennsylvania, where she expressed her distaste for party politics by registering as a Republican.

Pat needed volunteers (or draftees) to coach all these PRAC teams. She managed a girl's softball team on which Krista played very well, and persuaded me to join her staff, coaching a game I had never played. I tried my best, but I know I must have embarrassed Krista when the little girls in the outfield laughed at my inability to bat a ball, even when I tossed it into the air myself.

I coached football with greater success, first for Paul's team and then for little John's. Paul was a big, strong boy for his age, with the physical skills for football, but he was really not into the sport. John was a fierce competitor, fast and wiry, but he was a little guy for his age group. They both played well within their own capabilities.

Although my own sons drew me into coaching, I became involved in the development of scores of boys and learned valuable lessons about teaching and motivating youngsters. For example, in my first year as a coach I was so concerned about kids having fun that I suppressed my own competitiveness, discovering in that year of disappointing scores that "losing is no fun." The next year we became more disciplined and more focused on success, with great results. Kids don't have to win every competition to enjoy sports, but they do need always to believe that winning is possible for them and they need actually to win their fair share.

My experience in coaching football involved young boys, but girls were also eligible to play. Just to make that point, Krista showed up for practice one day in a football uniform and joined the scrimmage against the starting team. Like her father, she lined up on defense as a nose guard, directly in front of a big boy who was our starting center. "You've got a lot of guts, Krista," he growled just before he snapped the ball. She did have a lot of courage, but it was enough to prove that fact in just one day of football. Krista had already proven her athletic skills in softball, soccer, and basketball.

As Pat and I became increasingly involved in coaching young people, we rekindled our own interests in physical conditioning. In elementary school Pat had been the fastest runner in her class, so when the "running for health" movement swept America in the late 1970s she was eager to join the fun. I held back until I attended a Columbia seminar and was assured that it's okay to run badly, which is the only way I could ever run. We both became dedicated joggers around the high school track and Pat completed ten-mile runs on occasion.

The Park Ridge Athletic Club did not have a wrestling program when we arrived in 1976. Soon thereafter the Van Horn family moved into our community with three sons who had participated successfully on well-established youth wrestling teams in Oklahoma. Their sons bracketed John in both age and weight, and soon all four boys were appealing to PRAC to establish a wrestling team to compete with teams from other New Jersey towns. I was the only father remotely qualified to coach wrestling, so that was part of the deal. Other dads volunteered to help and Pat agreed to join me. She had watched me wrestle for seven years and she knew the sport technically. Pat was great with the littlest boys, cheering their best efforts and wiping their tears when necessary. She also became the team's chief organizer, dealing with attendance, schedules, and tournament logistics. (When the loudspeaker at a tournament called out for "Coach Likins" to come to the head table, they meant Pat, not me.)

Wrestling practice could not begin until I came home from work at Columbia, and that was too late for the youngest of the boys who wanted to wrestle. (A few girls wrestled very well on opposing teams, but none volunteered in Park Ridge.) To accommodate the first and second graders, Pat (with John) offered wrestling practice in the afternoon, and some little wrestlers coached only by her won district championships. She arranged exhibition bouts with the little brothers of her wrestlers, some only four years old, and concluded those matches with blue ribbons and hands raised in victory for both wrestlers, with everyone in the gym cheering loudly. Pat cherishes her "Thanks Coach" plaque even today.

The wrestling program became a big part of our lives in Park Ridge, consuming every weekday evening and most weekends throughout the winter months with as many as seventy-five wrestlers ranging in age from five to fourteen. John and his new friends from Oklahoma racked up several New Jersey state championships for their age and weight classes. We even took these four boys to a national championship tournament in Nebraska, where John came in fifth in just his second year of wrestling. (Pat would insist that I acknowledge flying to that tournament and flying back to work, leaving the joys of driving across the country with four rambunctious boys to their mothers.) The whole family was excited about John's spectacular success in the sport of wrestling, but among our children Teresa was John's biggest fan.

When you coach children for athletic competition, you want them to learn to win with humility and lose with grace. Both are important lessons in life, which never affords unremitting success in any venture. A good coach wants his or her athletes to exert every effort for victory, and still be able to lose with dignity and honor intact. This is not an easy lesson for a child, but there is no better time to learn.

John seemed to absorb these lessons naturally. He was a fierce competitor on the mat but affable and easygoing between matches, even hanging out with past or prospective opponents in the idle hours that dominate long tournaments. John rarely lost a match and was never pinned in competition, but he was always ready for a challenge and was not afraid to lose. The best evidence of John's character as a wrestler came about in a surprising way.

Before the Park Ridge team scheduled a wrestling match with a team from another town, the coaches conferred in detail, trying to arrange a positive wrestling experience for every kid who wanted to participate. We didn't keep team scores, but individual matches were won or lost.

A compassionate coach in a neighboring town asked if our 75-pound wrestler would wrestle a mentally challenged boy who had never wrestled before, just to give him a positive experience. Our wrestler agreed to do it until he saw the boy, who was visibly clumsy in his movements and obviously slow in other ways too. With the gym full of people, our 75-pound wrestler couldn't face the embarrassment of going out there with "that retard." John had just finished his match at 65 pounds and he volunteered to wrestle again.

The match that followed was a beautiful demonstration of the purest spirit of our son as a competitor. John made the wrestling feel real to his opponent, falling down with the boy on top, rolling around for dramatic effect, and finally going to his back to be pinned for the first (and only) time in his life. Both boys had a great experience that day. I have never been more proud of my son. His compassion for that mentally handicapped boy is particularly meaningful to me in retrospect; when John much later became mentally impaired himself, he was not always shown the same respect.

# 6

# The Lehigh Years

## Lehigh University

Pat called me in my office at Columbia one day in 1981, bubbling with excitement: "Pete, Lehigh University wants you to be a candidate for president!" She remembers well my response: "Honey, I'm still trying to figure out how to be a provost."

I was keenly aware of Lehigh's reputation, which was exceptionally strong in areas that matched my own profile. Lehigh University was one of five schools recommended by my Stanford faculty for graduate study in structural engineering: MIT, Illinois, Stanford, UC Berkeley, and Lehigh. My Tau Beta Pi fellowship could have been applied anywhere and I chose MIT, but I knew that Tau Beta Pi, the national engineering honor society that awarded my fellowship, had been founded at Lehigh. I also knew that Lehigh's wrestling tradition was arguably the best in the East and the best among private universities anywhere. My personal background in structural engineering and wrestling made me see Lehigh in a very positive light, but at forty-five years of age, with fewer than six years of administrative experience behind me, I wasn't sure that I was ready for a university presidency.

Pat was sure that I was ready and in good time the Lehigh trustees agreed. After preliminary interviews and my first visit to campus, I was eager for the challenge. I told the chair of the search committee that I would accept the position if offered, but I wanted to be sure that the trustees understood my family situation. I knew that Lehigh's culture was more conservative politically than Columbia's and I wanted the trustees to understand that I would share their fiscal conservatism but might stretch their tolerance when it came to "progressive" social policies. They hired me anyway.

I served as Lehigh's president for fifteen years and I will always have a special love for that university. This book is not the place for me to describe the very successful evolution of that institution from an excellent engineering college to a fine university with additional strengths in the arts and sciences, business, and education, but that goal was pushed hard and largely achieved.

The changes in the Lehigh student body over my fifteen years are more relevant to the story of my family for the parallels to be found. What I learned from my children helped me to serve my students and what I learned from my students helped me to raise my children.

When I assumed the Lehigh presidency in 1982, three-quarters of the students were able to pay the substantial tuition without financial aid or part-time work; more than half were engineering majors; only one in four was female; and students of color totaled about 10 percent of the student body (about 2 percent black, as I recall). I was concerned about this demographic profile for two stated reasons: (1) As a business proposition it seemed unsustainable to be limited in attracting students to that increasingly small minority consisting of affluent white males interested in engineering. (2) In recognition of the powerful demographic and societal trends in America, and the degree to which students learn from each other, it seemed likely to be increasingly difficult to provide an excellent education for the real world to any group of students as homogeneous as those being attracted to Lehigh at that time.

Every university president faces a multitude of challenges every day and most people (including trustees and regents) evaluate a president's performance on the basis of his or her success in meeting these constantly changing secondary challenges. A president's conscientious self-evaluation is, however, based on different criteria that address the question: "Am I helping my university improve its prospects for success in the long term?" By historical criteria, Lehigh was an absolutely splendid institution when I arrived in 1982, and its alumni and friends in industry were wonderfully supportive. While appreciating its virtues as my background uniquely prepared me to do, I felt that Lehigh's success was not sustainable in the long term without significant diversification of its academic strengths and its student population. Changes in university cultures cannot be commanded by their presidents, but they can evolve over time in ways their presidents can significantly influence. Lehigh's culture did change in the course of my fifteen years of service and it continues to evolve positively under the fine guidance of the current president, Alice Gast.

This book is not about presidential leadership, but it is about the evolution of society's values. Lehigh remains by many measures a relatively conservative academic institution with special strengths in engineering and applied science, but under the guidance of its trustees and academic leadership it has evolved in ways that reflect and often advance the changing character of American society. The trustees chose to stretch the university's traditions by deciding to admit women to its freshman class in 1971, by engaging in 1982 a president with an interracial family, and again by engaging as president in 2007 a distinguished engineering professor from the MIT leadership team who is also a woman. One can see the thirty-six-year span between the first female freshman and the first female president as rapid progress or slow, but this is undeniably progress determined by the Lehigh trustees. With each step on this long journey the trustees accepted risk and earned their rewards.

A large, full-color photograph of Lehigh University's new president and his family appeared in the summer of 1982 in the very first issue of the local newspaper to print in color. Lehigh is situated on a beautiful, wooded campus in Bethlehem, Pennsylvania, home of the once-powerful Bethlehem Steel Company, which dominated the culture both at the country-club level and in the working-class, ethnic neighborhoods that housed generations of steelworkers. One might expect a stiffening of the entire community in response to the colorful introduction of my family, but we never sensed any reluctance to accept us as we were. Probably we were perceived as a bit eccentric, as professors are permitted to be, but we were not rejected anywhere.

As president of the university I was automatically a member of the exclusive Saucon Valley Country Club, which had never had a black member. We were unaware of any concern about our black children at dances or in the swimming pool, and in time that club accepted a black member whom I sponsored, supported by colleagues in industry with greater country-club clout than I could muster.

Were there issues in the community relating to my family that were invisible to me? Perhaps so, but we didn't dwell on that possibility. Our daughter Krista may have felt some anxiety, however, when she first enrolled at Bethlehem Catholic High School as the only black girl in her class. She told other students that her father worked at the university as a janitor.

Lehigh is a private, residential university of focused academic programs and modest size, more on the model of Princeton or Dartmouth than that of Columbia. With about 4,500 undergraduates and 1,500 graduate students enrolled full time in just four colleges, it is small

~ *Pennsylvania family with Teresa still in New Jersey (1982). Left to right: Lora, Linda, John, Paul, Krista, Pat, and Pete. (Bethlehem Globe-Times photo, c. July 1982; used by permission of the Express-Times.)*

enough for Lehigh's president to spend quality time with students, both in the classroom and in extracurricular activities. I made a special effort to be a personal presence for Lehigh's small population of students of color, and I learned as much from them as they learned from me.

I was able to learn so much from them because they trusted me with their thoughts. I'm sure they knew that I had an interracial family, so I didn't have to tell them; they knew that I was safe. For my part, I wasn't burdened by the guilt hang-ups that compromise the effectiveness of so many well-meaning white liberals; because I loved my children I could shrug off any accusations or inferences of racist behavior.

When I expressed reservations about the establishment of the Umoja House ("umoja" is the Swahili word for "unity"), where black students could hang out and a few could reside, a black student leader made an appointment to see me so he could help me to understand their need for a place free of interracial tension. I came to see his perspective and approved the project.

When I accepted an invitation from a faculty colleague (Dr. Patti Ota) to co-teach a freshman seminar that was designed to help new students understand and respect the differences in the cultures of their fellow students in that deliberately diverse class, I welcomed the opportunity to engage those young people, including international students as well as Americans of black, Hispanic, and Asian background. The students participated openly in the seminar conversations and learned a great deal about various cultures, and they also quietly registered their impressions of each class meeting in a journal shared after each week with the faculty. A beautiful young woman of Puerto Rican heritage made an observation in her journal that conveyed a message more powerful than any provided by her teachers: "We've been talking for six weeks about all the ways we are different. Can we now talk about all the ways we are the same?"

Sometimes, as above, I learn from my students, and sometimes I learn with my students. As an example, I was approached in my office by two students, a man and a woman, who wanted me to add a club for gays and lesbians to the roster of university-sponsored clubs for Lehigh students. After discussing the options, we agreed that they would announce the creation of such a club as their own initiative, expecting loud but futile protests from local religious leaders and perhaps a few university trustees. They were, of course, within their incontestable legal rights to convene freely, so they would not be deterred by criticism. I promised to add their club to the roster of sponsored student groups after one year, and that I did without being rebuked. The students understood that I was more vulnerable to retribution than they were and they had the courage to take the heat. They trusted me and we accomplished our shared objective. Honest dialogue makes possible this kind of pragmatic strategy for progress as an alternative to public protestation of my failure to comply with their initial request.

On the other hand, public protest is sometimes the only available option for young people who feel the need to confront what they perceive as social injustice. When students came to me on occasion at Lehigh seeking guidance in choosing a strategy for advancing social change, I advised them candidly: "You have two legitimate options, and either is okay with me. If your intention is merely to call attention to injustice, your best strategy might be to protest loudly and publicly, but do not expect with this tactic actually to overcome the injustice. If your goal is actually to end the behavior you regard as unjust, the best strategy is to work within the system, exercising persuasion and well-placed power. Whatever you do, remember that you will not advance your cause if you sacrifice your own integrity or endanger other human beings."

There came a time in my Arizona presidency when the condition of respecting public safety was violated and I engaged the police immediately, but that was never necessary at Lehigh.

The practice of racial apartheid in South Africa provides an example of an injustice that presented Lehigh students with the dilemma of choosing a strategy to express their opposition. Unable to protest apartheid directly with any effect, they objected to university endowment investments in American companies doing business in South Africa. Although Lehigh's trustees listened thoughtfully to carefully articulated student appeals, they were not persuaded of the need to change investment policies. The protesting students then resorted to public demonstration by setting up a tent on campus for a "camp-out," occupied twenty-four hours a day as a center for speeches and the distribution of literature. I stopped by every morning on my daily jog, soon after 6 a.m., just to let them know that their university respected their right to demonstrate as long as no one got hurt and classes continued without interruption.

Gradually I was learning that my own growing responsibilities as a university president enabled me to reach beyond my family in the quest for social justice, but I also understood that the old Dr. Seuss story about "running the zoo" was pure fantasy. There were real limits on what I could do and how fast I could do it.

I have often drawn upon the social-change metaphor of stretching a fabric into a new shape, realizing that most fabrics can be stretched quite a bit if they are reshaped sufficiently slowly. When I stretch the social fabric I listen very carefully for the sounds of incipient ripping, stopping just short of rending the material. That's the way I maximize social change without unnecessary damage. Others may prefer to tear the social fabric deliberately, but then they find that weaving it back together again in the newly desired shape is a difficult, time-consuming, and unpredictable process.

At Lehigh I tried to expand the reach and range of the institution in every way that was consistent with the preservation of established standards of excellence. The campus doubled in size, new academic dimensions emerged, and the social culture was transformed. Over the course of fifteen years and with the collaboration of allies among the students, faculty, community, alumni, and trustees, we stretched the university quite significantly without tearing its fabric.

## Pennsylvania Family

The Lehigh University President's House was built of quarry stone in 1868 and it stands today magnificently at the heart of the campus. The President's Office in the Alumni Building is literally a small stone's throw from the house, so from my office window on the second floor I could see across the lawn to the kitchen window of my family home. After twenty years of commuting to work in Los Angeles and New York City, I appreciated the opportunity to merge work time with family time at Lehigh.

The old house has three floors aboveground and a full basement below. Social and ceremonial affairs were confined to the ground floor, with family living space on the second floor and a third floor for the kids (obviously intended originally for live-in servants). The basement included a laundry room, a "coal-room" accessible from outside, multiple storerooms, and a large, central room that was in our time covered by wrestling mats. Firewood was stacked in the coal-room to fuel three fireplaces on the main floor. Remembering the two-room cabin in which I grew up in Paradise Park and the single room that Pat and I had shared in Boston, I had a hard time believing that this was now our family home.

One night soon after we moved into this big, old house, with its unfamiliar elegance, John came down from his top-floor bedroom reporting the smell of smoke, which he had traced to an electrical outlet near his bed. The entire family was alerted, and the smell of smoke was detected in several places in the house, emanating from apertures in the walls, with no evidence of actual fire anywhere. We called the fire department and both kids and pets were gathered for quick escape.

Before the firefighters arrived, John discovered that the ceiling was burning in the basement coal-room, directly above the stacks of firewood. The firefighters axed the floor immediately above the burning ceiling and found fire occupying the generous space between floor and ceiling near a fireplace and extending to the interior of the wall by that fireplace, where electrical short circuits had sparked the fire initially.

Disaster was averted for both the family and that historic building, but our awareness of the deteriorating insulation on old wires took some of the romance out of living in that mansion, which was to be our home for fifteen years.

Visitors unfamiliar with the campus often came to the front door of the house seeking information, and early one morning a bold parent opened the door and found Pat in the kitchen in her robe and slippers. Undeterred, the visitor asked for directions to the admissions office. The Lehigh President's House was a very public place and the Lehigh presidency was embedded in the Lehigh Valley culture. We learned to live in a fishbowl, which was sometimes fun but not always.

An undergraduate residence hall was uphill and across a small street from the President's House and the music from student loudspeakers reverberated across the space between. We soon discovered that our kids had set up their own speakers on the top floor, directed toward the Lehigh students, enjoying their own version of the battle of the bands.

Our master bedroom overlooked that same street as it wound around our house to reach the students' rooms, and late at night it was not unusual to hear drunken students serenading their president, signing off with "Goodnight, Pete." I would roll over in bed with a smile, but Pat was not so happy with the disturbance. She put a "For Sale" sign in our front yard.

Relationships with students at Lehigh were well integrated into our daily family living. We often had student receptions in the house, so our own children were interacting with college students. We all attended Lehigh football games, wrestling matches, and other athletic events, as well as the high school sports involving our own children, so the memories all run together.

Our kids also met some very interesting guests of the university at gatherings in our home.

When the Soviet wrestling team came to the United States to meet our All-Star team, the opposing wrestlers competed in Lehigh's arena and socialized afterward at the President's House. Our son John, the wrestler, had a unique experience.

When Bill Cosby came to campus for a commencement address, Krista was thrilled to sit across from him at our luncheon table, even though he teased her unmercifully.

When Lehigh alumnus Lee Iacocca, head of Chrysler Corporation at the time, sat down with us in our family room after his commencement address, Lora was late to arrive, having been squeezed into a campus bus for the ride from the commencement venue. She burst into the room exclaiming, "That bus was as crowded as our family all together in our Honda!"

"Honda?" said Lee. "Honda?"

I quickly explained to the hero of the American auto industry that we no longer owned a Honda. (I didn't mention the Subaru parked next to our Dodge van in the garage.)

When members of the Lehigh cross-country team discovered that their president was featured in a *Runner's World* article on executives who jog for stamina and stress relief, they asked to join me on my morning run. I told them to meet me at my customary time (6 a.m.) for my customary run (to the top of South Mountain and back, two miles) and I insisted that they run backwards (a demand I rescinded when they actually showed up on schedule). They patiently jogged along with me until I made it back home, and then they sprinted into their real workout for the morning.

Although all six Likins kids were assigned their own bedrooms in that big house when I began my Lehigh presidency, only the three youngest children were then living at home and going to school in the community: Linda, Krista, and John. By the time I concluded my Lehigh presidency fifteen years later, all the kids were out of the house and the third floor served as a shelter for special cats Pat fostered for the SPCA. Even before the outset of my presidency, however, Teresa, Lora, and Paul had graduated from high school and left the family nest, at least for the time being.

Teresa had begun nursing training in New Jersey, and she stayed at the hospital in a supportive role when she dropped out of the RN program. She did not make the move to Pennsylvania with the family, and lived a rather private life for several years. We saw her only occasionally, and no one in the family knew that she was pregnant until she announced on June 5, 1988, the birth of a son she named Thomas Peter Likins. We never met the father, whom she lightly described as "a passing Irishman." (Whoever he was, we came later to realize that he had contributed fine genes to the union.) Pat encouraged Teresa to come home with her baby, who became the shared responsibility of all the women in the Likins household.

Pat and I returned from the NCAA wrestling tournament in the spring of 1990 to a surprising announcement from Teresa and Lora: They planned to switch roles in Tommy's life. Lora would become the baby's adoptive mother and Teresa would play the role of his aunt. When we wondered aloud how this would actually work out, we were told that the decision had been made. In retrospect, we came to recognize the wisdom of this decision by our two daughters.

Lora was the perfectionist among our children, the little girl whose only shortcoming was her penchant for trying too hard. Pat and I were very much aware that we had to strike a balance between asking too much and asking too little of our individual children, each of whom responded differently to our attempts at motivation. Lora did everything we asked of her, and then tried to do a little more. She was a serious student and responsible in her social life—the perennial "designated driver" in high school and college. We worried about her because parents always worry.

Lora showed an early interest in deaf education and when she graduated from Park Ridge High School she enrolled in a speech pathology and audiology program at Ithaca College in New York. She was away from home, but still within a day's drive from our new home in Pennsylvania. She had a good experience at Ithaca College, but she shifted direction after graduation and enrolled for a master's degree in a "social relations" program at Lehigh, writing her thesis on deaf education. Although her degree was in sociology, not social work, she managed to get a job as a social worker in nearby Carbon County, working for Children and Youth Services. She took that job to place needy children for adoption, but harsh reality took her to court more often to testify against abusive parents. Lora had always been responsible, but in Carbon County she grew strong.

Over the years Lora's work plan took her from teaching to social work to nursing; she earned her nursing diploma at St. Luke's Hospital in Bethlehem and worked in hospitals and doctor's offices there for some years.

Lora had married soon after her college graduation, somehow feeling that she should do what her classmates were doing. She adopted Thomas, Teresa's birth child, in that marriage, but the relationship never had the foundations required for marital survival. Lora and Tom were soon on their own.

Lora became quite a self-sufficient young woman and she was prepared to raise her little boy on her own, with a little help from others in the family. Then Frank Woods came into her life, and in time Lora and her son moved to Rhode Island to be with Frank, whose two children by a previous marriage were important elements of the newly gathering

*⌁ Nurse Lora (1994). (School photo.)*

family. At the University of Rhode Island Lora earned both her bachelor's and her master's degree in nursing, so by that time she had two bachelor's and two master's degrees to her name. She was prepared to be either a teacher, a social worker, or a nurse, covering most of the "caring professions." She taught a course on clinical practice to nursing students at the University of Rhode Island, she worked for a time as a school nurse, and she practiced in a clinical setting. Lora seemed always to enjoy learning, continuing her formal education, both in person and online, at every opportunity. In her mid-forties at this writing, she is still moving in new directions on her own initiative, responding to her need to search for and maybe find the most felicitous path through life.

Paul followed Lora to Ithaca College one year later, but with very different results. As noted previously, Paul failed defiantly in his first two attempts at college, winding up in Manhattan during these transitional years, seeking an identity in photography or rock music or whatever passion drove him relentlessly. Paul was a handsome young man with a good mind going to waste, and Pat and I were both confused and disappointed. What had we done wrong?

When Paul's behavior at eighteen stretched my patience beyond my narrow limits, I asked Lora the question that had been lingering in my mind: "Is Paul gay?"

"Ask him, Dad," was her wise reply.

After Paul and I had that conversation, sadly five years later than a more worldly father would have chosen, the wounds in our relationship began to heal. In time the bonds between us grew stronger than they had ever been, finally forging a father-son relationship that is both mutually respectful and genuinely affectionate. That was not an easy journey.

I have always regretted that in my ignorance I left my son to struggle all alone as an adolescent with the complexities of his own sexual identity. Pat was way ahead of me in sensing without words what Paul was going through, but she waited for him to open the door to that conversation, and she waited too long.

At some point Paul faced harsh reality and declared himself to Alcoholics Anonymous as an alcoholic, abstaining completely from alcohol and other drugs. (He wouldn't even eat a bite of rum cake.) Without any of the usual relapses of recovering addicts, Paul began to rebuild his life on his own terms. He started college again at the Borough of Manhattan Community College, did so well that he earned a scholarship at New York University, and in his mid-thirties graduated with honors in the field of communications. Pat and I had moved to Arizona by that time, but I was proud to attend his graduation ceremonies. Paul benefited from psychotherapy in New York and restored what had been a strained (but never estranged) relationship with both of his parents.

Moving beyond the story of my family during our Pennsylvania years, Paul followed us to Arizona and enrolled in a master's degree program in communications at the University of Arizona, where he had full responsibility as a teaching assistant for an undergraduate class. He was remarkably successful as a teacher at the UA, receiving teaching evaluations from his students that were deeply gratifying. Although he was doing well in his courses, Paul found the emphasis on social science research at the UA less appealing than the NYU approach to communications, so he transferred back to NYU and earned his master's degree there.

While attending NYU, Paul got a job at CBS Marketwatch in online advertising, a new field of endeavor that offered a young person great

~ *Paul and his father (2010). (Family photo.)*

opportunities. This work continued after graduation with experience in New York and San Francisco at several firms, including Time Inc., Rodale Press, and the *Wall Street Journal*, where at this writing he is thriving with management responsibilities. Finally we can share perspectives on life and work, discovering that we have some common views on both. Paul told me once that his management style is that of a teacher, not realizing that I would say the same thing for myself. Pat and I can see that Paul is on a good path, both personally and professionally. We are all greatly pleased when Paul treats his parents to a Broadway show in New York, reversing roles dramatically.

With Teresa, Lora, and Paul mostly out of the house, we had three kids to worry about in Pennsylvania: Linda, Krista, and John.

Linda moved out of the "special ed" environment to join the mainstream of students at Bethlehem Catholic High School ("Becahi"), from which she graduated in 1984. She was a lovable girl, easily guided and always wanting to please. We were apprehensive about the possibility of inherited vulnerability to alcohol, and on one occasion we were alarmed by her imbibing as much as my brother and I did one night in our early teens, with the same body-purging consequences, but this turned out to be an isolated event. Linda took better care of herself than most teenagers. She maintained her slim but mature figure by incessant exercise. She was a reliable performer with her clarinet in the very impressive high school marching band. Linda enjoyed friends several years younger than she was, but this was the only reminder of her delayed development. Among her younger friends was a boy with whom she maintained a steady relationship right through his years as an engineering student at Penn State University and his graduate student years at Lehigh. Linda developed a surprisingly solid sense of herself, crawling out of the very deep hole in which she was nearly buried as a seven-year-old to become a responsible, self-sufficient young adult. After high school she had a succession of jobs in health care, proudly passing the tests to become a licensed practical nurse on her own initiative. Pat and I realized that she was still a very malleable personality, so willing to please that she was vulnerable to the darker forces in life, but we were very proud of Linda's progress during our fifteen years in Pennsylvania.

Krista was always a beautiful child with an engaging personality. Athletics had been important to her sense of herself in New Jersey, and in high school she played soccer and softball, but with diminishing enthusiasm. Krista made friends easily and she faced life with a winning smile. She had great fun with her girlfriends, who at Becahi were all white, but was hurt by subtle racial slights on more than one occasion.

Picture a gaggle of laughing high school girls crowding through the doorway of a pizza parlor when the girls in front reverse direction and lead their puzzled friends back onto the sidewalk. "We can't go in there," says one girl. "There's nobody in there but black people." Then, "Oh, sorry, Krista. I don't think of you as black."

Imagine a Catholic priest telling his high school class about his origins in Italy, asking his students the friendly question, "How many of you are at least partly of Italian descent?" When Krista (whose birth mother was of Polish and Italian heritage) raised her hand, the priest dismissed her as a joke: "You can't be part Italian, Krista."

To a degree not entirely apparent at the time, Krista was sometimes managing some of the more difficult issues in her life by suppressing painful realities and living joyfully in the moment. She was perceived as a cheerful girl with a positive attitude, but she was laughing at times to avoid confronting hurtful experiences. Krista had a difficult time focusing on her studies and became self-conscious about her performance in the classroom. She had friends who were boys, but no long-term boyfriends in high school. We were aware that she was for a time the only black girl in her class at Becahi and we allowed her for this primary reason to transfer to the public Liberty High School. There she found that she was not black enough for the other black girls, either in her appearance or in her speech. She tangled at a local dance with some black girls, who seemed to resent any competition for the black guys who might be interested in Krista. We knew that she wasn't always happy, but she managed to slide by with her radiant smile and self-deprecating humor, which worked well enough for her in high school to permit admission to a local Catholic college, St. Francis de Sales (now de Sales University), where she majored in dramatics.

As a freshman, Krista was told by her drama teacher, a priest, that he didn't have many "black roles." Krista changed her major to psychology and drifted uninspired through four years of college, dropping out without a degree. Her grades were okay when she was living at home during summer sessions, but living on campus held too many distractions for this fun-loving girl, who had lost her aspirational motivations and couldn't stay focused on her studies. She took a job in a child-care center on campus, where she was warmly received and well regarded.

Krista was unprepared for the young men who entered her life as she grew older, too easily impressed by a handsome guy and too slow to see beneath the surface. Krista always tried to charm her way to survival, and in this she often succeeded—often, but not always. Despite the exceptional promise of her early years, the skies were darkening for Krista in the later years of family life in Pennsylvania.

As the youngest of our six children, and in some ways the most challenging in early childhood, John had received more than his fair share of parental attention. By the time he entered Bethlehem Catholic High School, however, he was on the right track. Years of parental "investment" of time and loving care seemed to be paying off for John, who was by then a good student, a superb athlete, and remarkably self-assured in his relationships with peers and adults. He was a popular guy on campus, adding to his reputation as an athlete by performing an exciting break-dance on the stage at a school performance. John was unusually open in his communications with his parents, especially with his mother, talking, for example, about sexual relationships with candor. He could be counted on to tell the truth, even if it hurt, as it often did. John didn't

~ *John and his father (2002). (Family photo by Patti Ota.)*

always stay out of trouble, but he was never rebellious or angry in his demeanor. Like Krista, John was a charmer, but his winning ways seemed to rest on a more secure foundation.

John was badly shaken when he realized at seventeen that he had conceived a child with a classmate. The new mother was a remarkably strong and mature young woman, eager to have her new daughter adopted by the fine couple that Pat had recommended. Both families of the biological parents attended the baby's birth, and John was able, however briefly, to hold the child he had created before she was swept away for a better life than either parent could provide.

I will have more to say later about John's wrestling, which continued to be central to his life in high school. He won the Pennsylvania State Wrestling Championship in his junior year, assuring him of a college scholarship at the University of Pittsburgh, where he was preceded by his Becahi teammate and future national champion Pat Santoro (who later became the head wrestling coach at Lehigh). John was on a clear path to an NCAA championship if he could match Pat's determination and resolve.

Soon after his dramatic success at the state tournament in the spring of 1986, the bottom dropped out for John. As his parents, we felt that the bottom had dropped out of our lives as well. Always vigilant, Pat discovered a marijuana pipe in John's back pocket, which we found shocking. John was too dedicated an athlete to smoke cigarettes and he seemed no more likely than I had been to get into trouble with alcohol. But John's use of alcohol as a sedative was disturbing to us, and the discovery of his marijuana use was alarming. We tried desperately to intervene, but John accelerated quickly to cocaine, stunning everyone who thought they knew him well.

John's triumphs and tragedies became triumphs and tragedies for the entire family, as I will try to describe a bit later.

## Wrestling

John's interest in wrestling and his natural aptitude for the sport stirred in me feelings that were much deeper than mere memories of my own youthful exploits. My success as a wrestler, although modest by the highest national standards, had been a formative influence on my development. I've been quoted often for declaring that I learned to be a university president on the wrestling mats, and that was not just university humor. The wrestler's capacity for discipline, resolve, resilience, and equanimity in conflict serves any university president well.

At Lehigh, where the wrestling tradition is very deep, my reputation as a former wrestler soon eclipsed any actual achievements I could claim, and in my fifties even those successes were far behind me. Nonetheless, I was unable to refuse a challenge match with one of Lehigh's distinguished trustees, Kirk Pendleton, to be televised in advance of a Lehigh team match. Kirk was a former NCAA champion who had lost only two matches in his entire Lehigh wrestling career. He was also younger, stronger, and in better shape than I was, but I knew he would try not to inflict any permanent damage. My wife Pat worked his corner and his wife Carolyn covered mine.

We agreed to a three-minute match with no script but with a mutual pledge to avoid any blocking, defensive moves so the action would be exciting. Until the final minute I was taking a beating, behind one to five, when in avoiding blocking moves Kirk fell into the unusual hold I called the Hitchcock; I reversed control and put him on his back, good for five additional points as the final whistle blew. The match ended in a six to six

~ *Pete at Lehigh (inset) and with Kirk in a "Hitchcock" (c. 1991).*
*(Lehigh University photo.)*

tie, thanks to the diplomacy of referee Mike Caruso, a three-time national
champion who later became a Lehigh trustee himself. Mike gave Kirk a
point at the end of the match "on general principles."

I dragged myself out of bed the next morning and tape-recorded a
memo: "Ten reasons to say NO next year," listing my ten most serious
injuries. Wrestling is not a physical activity that carries over well into
middle age, but the lessons learned in that sport last a lifetime.

A wrestler's purpose on the mat is to control his opponent. The
supreme manifestation of that control is the pin, with the opponent's
shoulder blades held on the mat. Wrestling can be a violent sport, but
it is not its purpose to inflict pain or cause injury; the purpose is body
control. Being pinned can cause humiliation, but that pain is mental.

Before a wrestler can control his opponent, he must exercise superb
control of himself. A young wrestler learns that he can control his weight
safely with diet and physical exercise, a lesson that can last a lifetime.
As Pat and I learned in coaching youth wrestling, a wrestler who gets

mad usually gets beat. Emotional intensity and fierce focus can improve performance, but a wrestler who loses his temper almost always loses his match as well. A wrestler learns to control his emotions in combat, so his adrenaline jacks up his intensity without impairing his judgment. This is another of life's valuable lessons.

A successful wrestler is almost always blessed with a natural ability to sense the position of his entire body in relation to that of his opponent. Blind wrestlers with this ability are not seriously handicapped in this sport. This body-control capability is a differentiating talent that can be observed in a ten-year-old novice wrestler. Training can make a wrestler stronger and smarter on the mat, and maybe a little bit quicker, but no amount of practice develops that magical capacity for body control.

Mental toughness is another quality with lifelong value that differentiates one great wrestler from another. The Pete Schuyler story defines the concept.

When Pete Schuyler was a senior at Lehigh, he was considered the second-best wrestler in America at 137 pounds. The best wrestler was John Whalen of Missouri, who had defeated Pete repeatedly. When they entered their final NCAA Championship Tournament, Pete was seeded second, determined to beat his old nemesis (the top seed) in the finals.

To reach the championship match in the finals, both Pete and John had to win several difficult matches. In his semifinal match, Pete was leading a tough kid from Iowa by only one point with eight seconds remaining. With the Iowa wrestler flat on his belly, however, totally unable even to get to his knees under Pete's dominating ride, it seemed that a win was assured. The referee decided at that moment to blow his whistle, charging Pete with stalling because he was not trying hard enough to turn his opponent on his back, as the rules require. After the whistle, the wrestlers returned to their starting position on their knees, with Pete in control on top. In the eight seconds remaining the Iowa wrestler reversed the Lehigh wrestler, earning two points and the victory. Pete Schuyler was denied his shot at John Whalen in the finals.

As legend has it, Pete Schuyler came off the mat after his crushing disappointment with the words, "Now I've gotta win the bronze for third." He was not railing at the referee for stealing his victory or moaning about his defeat; he was already getting prepared mentally for his next match.

And who was his opponent to be? His old nemesis, John Whalen, had also suffered a shocking defeat and would be wrestling for third.

Pete Schuyler won his battle with John Whalen for the third-place medal. Whalen may have been the better wrestler, but Pete Schuyler was mentally tougher. This is no reflection on John Whalen; Pete Schuyler was mentally tougher than almost anyone.

Few qualities better predict success in life than resilience, the ability to bounce back quickly from a bad experience. Everyone takes a hit now and then, and a certain mental toughness is necessary for quick recovery and agile response. The Pete Schuyler story is not about wrestling.

Although the sport of wrestling was very important to my own development, and I was very successful in the context of my competition, I quickly recognized in my son John a much higher level of natural aptitude. Pat and I have enjoyed reading ancient news clippings describing my "catlike quickness," but we both knew that this old cat was never as quick as his son.

John was a naturally gifted wrestler with a combination of quickness, strength, balance, and determination that enabled him to win multiple state championships as a youngster in New Jersey and a state high school championship in Pennsylvania, which is among the most competitive arenas in America. He almost always won, but he was not afraid to lose.

At the end of an undefeated dual-meet season in his sophomore year of high school, when virtually all wrestlers were dropping one weight class for tournament competition, John delayed his scheduled weight loss in order to meet an undefeated three-time state champion senior named Jack Cuvo (later a national collegiate champion) who was dropping into John's regular-season weight class for the tournament. John attacked aggressively and to everyone's surprise led after the first period, but Jack's incredible stamina enabled him to overcome John's superior effort in the second period, and by the time the third period was over Jack had won convincingly. (Jack was also a state champion in cross-country, an unusual combination with wrestling but one that also requires great stamina.)

As John was preparing to enter the series of state tournaments at the end of that sophomore year, the night before the District Championship Tournament he damaged some cartilage in his knee, and the torn cartilage jammed his knee joint so he could not bend it until the trainer stretched his leg to free the cartilage fragment. John entered the tournament anyway, stopped his matches as necessary for the trainer to unlock the knee joint, and won the tournament on a Saturday night. Arthroscopic surgery the next day removed the torn cartilage fragments from his knee, and he won the regional tournament the following Friday with his knee heavily

✎ *John wrestling for Becahi (c. 1988). (Family photo.)*

bandaged, qualifying for the state tournament. He placed fifth in the state that year, and was well prepared for the state tournament the following year. John won the Pennsylvania State Championship as a junior at 112 pounds. He was approached by college coaches with scholarship offers and he committed informally to the University of Pittsburgh, where his teammate, Pat Santoro, had gone before him.

As mentioned, John's life went into a tailspin at the end of his junior year, but he recovered from his drug problems to compete again successfully in his senior year. Rather than stay at 112 pounds, he decided to move up to 119 pounds, recognizing that 118 pounds was the lowest weight contested in college. The threatening obstacle at 119 pounds was a boy named Bob Truby who had not only won that weight class in Pennsylvania the preceding year but been named the tournament's "Outstanding Wrestler." John met Bob Truby in the finals in his senior year and was the aggressor throughout the match, but in wrestling the defensive strategy often prevails except at the highest levels; Truby won by a point or two in a fierce contest that was the talk of the tournament. Bob Truby became a successful wrestler at Penn State University, but his defensive style was not so effective at that level and the national championship eluded him.

After the wrestling season was over, John began struggling again with his addictions. One night he snuck out of the house by climbing down from the second floor on a drainpipe, and when he tried to return the same way he lost his grip and fell to the asphalt below, breaking his hand severely. We all wondered if he would ever regain sufficient use of that hand to return to wrestling, or if any college coach would take a chance on John.

Pitt's coach, Randy Stottlemeyer, stayed in John's corner, visiting him in the hospital and reaffirming his offer of a college scholarship. We all saw this generous offer as an opportunity for John to put his drug use behind him and return to wrestling as his salvation. John made the team's starting lineup as a freshman, but he disappeared into the dark streets of Pittsburgh just before Christmas vacation that year. It was the wrestling team that found John in that dangerous world as Pat and I rushed to Pittsburgh. John's wrestling years were over.

## Alcohol and Other Drugs

As the nation's "drug czar" in the 1980s, Bill Bennett invited a small group of college presidents to a private hearing in Washington, D.C., seeking counsel on strategies to combat drug abuse on college campuses. When we went around the table for testimony by individual presidents, every one of us independently characterized alcohol as the "drug of choice" on campus and the source of the greatest damage to individuals and institutions. This was not what Bennett wanted to hear because his focus was understandably on illegal drugs, beginning with marijuana. The meeting was not very productive.

The language we use to describe America's drug problem is often confused and confusing, but words are important. When we speak of "drugs" do we include all mind-altering substances, or merely those that are illegal? Do we mean to include only substances that are addictive? What about substances that seem to cause addiction for some individuals but not others? Are we dealing with mental illness or just bad behavior? Are we concerned about "drug abuse" or just "drug addiction"? And what do we mean by the terms "abuse" and "addiction"? Before we have any hope of solving a problem, we must learn how to talk about it in language we all understand.

If we use the term "drug" to describe any mind-altering substance, we have included a very wide variety of chemicals, some of which are medically prescribed or generally acceptable for social and recreational use. Alcohol is a drug by such a definition, but so is caffeine. I am comfortable with such a broad use of the term, but I use it in this way with no stigma attached. America's drug problem is not drug use but drug abuse, particularly by people addicted to certain substances.

When Mr. Bennett's panel of college presidents described alcohol as the number-one problem drug on campus, they were reporting widespread and dangerous use of alcohol to the point of extreme drunkenness and associated violent and destructive behavior, such as rape or assault. In general, they were reporting alcohol abuse, which only rarely was explained by yet-undiagnosed alcohol addiction.

I have often wondered about some of my college buddies at Stanford who seemed even then to drink excessively. Were they budding alcoholics? I do know of one example at Lehigh of a very impressive student leader who told me in his sophomore year that he needed alcohol to handle the pressures of student life, and told me years later at an alumni affair that he was then a recovering alcoholic. Alcoholism on campus can be veiled by the prevalence of hard drinkers who establish a false sense of what represents a "normal" amount of drinking.

I use the term "drug addict" to describe someone who chronically feels compelled to use drugs even with the knowledge that such use is destructive to the user and to other people who should matter to the user, such as friends and family. I see drug addiction as a chronic mental illness or brain malfunction that we do not yet understand in physiological terms and consequently cannot yet cure. As research into brain function yields better understanding of mental illnesses in all their variety and complexity, I expect addiction to be better understood in this context.

Alcohol seems to be a drug that can be used extensively by some people without addiction, but some people are rapidly addicted even in adolescence.

Nicotine seems to be almost universal in its powers of addiction, but the negative consequences of tobacco addiction are generally delayed and therefore less immediately destructive to the user and others.

Marijuana is potentially addictive by the definition used here, but it seems to be less powerful in its addictive grip than alcohol.

We are all sadly familiar with the litany of deadly drugs whose addicts populate our prisons and hospital emergency rooms, drugs like heroin, crack cocaine, and methamphetamines. Their destructive influence on our society is disproportionate to the numbers of users because of associated criminal behavior.

All of this talk is important in the creation of policies to manage drug use, both nationally and on individual college campuses. But these words are utterly useless to the parents of a child who becomes a drug addict. For those bereft souls there are no comforting words, only confusion, grief, and fear.

Somehow, our own childhood experiences with alcohol use and abuse didn't seem to help Pat and me to cope with our son's addiction. Both my father and Pat's stepfather were probably functioning alcoholics, although I didn't live with my father sufficiently to be sure that his continuous drinking truly implied a dependence and Pat's stepfather drank only rarely but then uncontrollably.

When Pat grew up in the 1950s, "good girls" didn't drink but boys who got drunk at parties were not condemned as their sisters would have been. Alcohol was generally not perceived as an addictive drug; only "weak" people became alcoholics. Other drugs, such as marijuana, were the stuff of stories about other people, not high school kids in Santa Cruz, California.

Pat did not use alcohol until after high school, and then only sparingly. Until my relationship with Pat got me back on a straight path, I acted as though I was determined to demonstrate with alcohol that I was "one of the boys," despite sterling grades and my high visibility in athletics and campus politics. Twice I ended up in jail for underage drinking before I was sixteen.

My brother Tod and I drank ourselves into a stupor one New Year's Eve when I was fourteen, consuming a potentially deadly mixture of straight bourbon and orange liqueur in eight-ounce glasses with our buddies from Paradise Park until we all passed out. I have never learned to enjoy bourbon.

The Paradise Park boys often hiked in the redwood forests or up the river for overnight camping, sometimes with our backpacks full of quart bottles of beer. I was the youngest of the group, but we were all under sixteen.

A beer party on the ocean beach near Santa Cruz got out of hand when I drank some vodka provided by older kids at their own beach party. My friends foolishly took me for coffee to a popular drive-in restaurant favored by the police, who witnessed a belligerent, drunken kid challenging an older boy from school. I was locked behind bars until my unhappy stepfather, who had only recently married my mother, came to rescue me. I was just fourteen.

After my football team won the league lightweight championship in my junior year of high school, when I was fifteen, the team and about thirty other kids convened at a farmhouse a few miles out of town for a gigantic celebration. Only when the party got busted did I realize that the farmhouse was "borrowed" without permission from its owners and the wine that filled the bathtub was stolen from another nearby farmhouse. The police roundup took my brother Tod and me to the sheriff's station, but there were too many wayward youth to fit in the jail cells. Our new stepfather must have been wondering what he had done in marrying our mother.

That stepfather, Paul Forgey, a decent man who was at the time mayor of Santa Cruz, suffered one more indignity before Tod and I left the household after high school graduation in 1953. After our junior year, at a time when our mother had taken the two younger children and joined her husband and his daughter for a brief vacation, Tod and I helped the graduating seniors celebrate by putting a sign prominently in the window of our home announcing that this was the place to be: "Party time all the time!" The next morning we cleaned up the evidence of the party and asked one of our buddies to discard the box of bottles. He stupidly dropped the box on a neighbor's lawn, not noticing that the box had the name "Paul Forgey" on its label. Mayor Forgey was mortified when the box was returned.

By the time I was sixteen, and serious about my future with Pat, all this nonsense was behind me. College still offered fraternity parties and alcohol, but never again did I lose control as I did too often in high school. Probably I consumed more alcohol before I was twenty-one than in the fifty years following.

With memories of my own youthful indiscretions with alcohol, I thought I was ready to be a father for teenagers. I was, however, unprepared for the change in behavior patterns of girls using alcohol and totally unprepared for the drugs other than alcohol that entered my family life.

We did recognize that our Indian children had special vulnerabilities to worry about. It is well known that American Indians are statistically vulnerable to alcoholism, and both of the birth parents of our two Indian girls faced early death in which alcohol was complicit, so we were apprehensive as first Teresa and then Linda entered the dangerous adolescent years. Teresa has not avoided alcohol and may have had more experience than we realized, but this has never seemed to be a special problem for her. Linda had the singular experience described previously that was reminiscent of my own introduction to potentially lethal levels of intoxication, but this kind of behavior did not endure. The two children who we thought might be most vulnerable have not been the most affected by alcohol.

Nor was Lora ever a concern. As noted, she was the "designated driver" among her partying friends. She was there with them but she was sober, or so we believe. Who knows why? Was her mother's example being deliberately followed, or is this a coincidence?

Paul had less trouble with alcohol in high school than I did, but it persisted longer and gradually escalated after he dropped out of college and found his way into a fast life in Manhattan. Paul tended bar on occasion and even managed a bar for a while, so alcohol and other drugs were part of his daily life. Nonetheless, it surprised Pat and me when Paul decided that he was an alcoholic and joined Alcoholics Anonymous. This was a critical turning point for Paul, and he never relapsed or fell back from his resolve to rebuild his life. It became apparent after two abstinent decades that alcohol was more a symptom of Paul's problems than a cause, but in facing his alcohol abuse problem he learned to deal with destructive behavior in all of its guises. Pat and I have always appreciated Paul's intelligence and his potential for achievement, so his success in conquering his demons and rebuilding his life meant a great deal to us.

Krista's experience in high school and college with alcohol and other drugs was probably typical for her generation. We did not recognize any problems until she was a young adult, exploring social relationships in new territory. For some human beings the path to addiction seems to be predetermined as a direct consequence of the initial use of addictive substances, but for others this is a gradual process that sets in only after years of incidental use of alcohol and other drugs. After Krista left the constraining influence of her home with us and entered the world as a young adult, her casual use of cocaine gradually became compelling. She began a downward spiral that led to serious crises in her life and sporadic attempts at rehabilitation. She found herself in the darkest of places as she approached her fortieth birthday and resolved to turn her life around.

⤳ *Krista with her mother and father (2010). (Family photo.)*

She completed a tough, five-month program at a Narconon facility and then completed with high marks a training program that enabled her to become a certified nursing assistant in California. I truly believe that she is now permanently on the right path. Her mental health is excellent and she is beautiful again, inside and out. Her recovery has been a great blessing for everyone in our extended family.

Finally we come to John's story, which was unique in our family from its beginning. John had the same adventures with beer parties that Paul, Tod, and I experienced, but he also drank alone. One afternoon Pat saw John drinking a large glass of "grape juice" in the living room while watching television and took it from him to spare the carpet from being stained by spills. She was astonished to discover that the glass held red wine.

As noted, John also gave Pat her introduction to marijuana. She found a marijuana pipe in his jeans and confronted him angrily. He seemed unconcerned. John accepted our insistence on counseling, and left his counselors puzzled. They saw John as a good kid with fine values, but he persisted in using alcohol and marijuana. In retrospect, we see that John's psychologist offered a clue that we did not catch; he said that there was something going on within John that he could not identify.

John escalated within a few months to snorting cocaine, which seemed to the people who thought they knew John as totally out of character. When Pat and I took John for the first time to a local hospital for drug detoxification, we both came down the elevator in tears.

John spent thirty days in an upscale drug rehabilitation center under the care of psychiatrists, nurses, social workers, and counselors. Within a week of his return home he was using again. He spent ninety days in a tougher environment in Erie, Pennsylvania, that was essentially run by recovering addicts, and returned home with every promise of staying away from drugs. He reentered high school at Becahi, led the wrestling team to the state tournament, and graduated with a wrestling scholarship to Pitt. He entered Pitt for summer session to begin his freshman year and when the wrestling season began he made the starting lineup immediately. He seemed to be on his way to the realization of all of his promise. However, before Christmas he relapsed again and Pat and I had to take him home to the Lehigh Valley for further treatment.

John was never a rebellious or angry young man. He always cooperated in his treatment, which nonetheless always ultimately failed. An example of John's complicity in our efforts to keep him clean defies belief, but it illustrates the craziness of our shared ordeal.

Remember that I was trying to do my job as a university president all this time. In that role I was chatting with guests at a dedication of new Lehigh facilities and thinking about the remarks I was expected to make in an hour when a campus police officer discreetly took me aside to inform me that my son John was in the campus lockup, high on drugs. I excused myself quietly and went to my son, who was quite rational by that time. Both John and I realized that he would bolt if set free, but I hated to leave him in our jail. John suggested that we borrow police handcuffs and lock him to his bed in the President's House until he came down from his high and I got back from my reception. This we did. I went back to my reception and gave my welcoming address. John was waiting patiently when I returned home to free him from his shackles.

The cycle of recovery and relapse continued, with each hospital detox followed by a rehab center whose promise ended in disappointment. John was scheduled to move from one such three-day detox to a thirty-day rehab when Lora was about to be married, and we all agreed that he could attend the wedding before going to the scheduled rehab. People who knew John's recent history were pleased to see him dancing happily at Lora's wedding reception. Even in his addiction, John was always charming and never radiated anger as disaffected children often do. Then John stole some of Lora's most valuable wedding gifts and disappeared into the streets of the Lehigh Valley.

Although Pat and I had never been secretive about John's affliction, we knew that if we reported John's theft to the police his arrest would be a headline story in the two local newspapers. Not only was John Likins the son of Lehigh's president, he was locally famous in his own right as a state wrestling champion. Nevertheless, we immediately called the police, who found John within a few days. John Likins in handcuffs made the front page.

The community reaction was quite surprising. I received a hundred letters, almost all reflecting the similar concerns of other parents in the Lehigh Valley, who seemed somehow relieved that even the president of the university shared their problems. Although the newspapers were simply factual in their reporting, both papers also printed a piece I had written with the intention of having it printed in the Lehigh alumni magazine. I knew that the story had to break soon and I had decided to break it myself. Lehigh's trustees were also quite understanding; they declined my offer to resign the presidency and urged me to stand my ground and face the issues directly. I did so.

John's theft landed him in jail, but the courts gave him the option of doing his time in a tough drug rehab center called Hogar Crea, which was run by addicts in recovery. John was there for some time and both Pat and I developed great respect for the men who made Hogar Crea work so well. This organization was first established in Puerto Rico, and many of the Lehigh Valley residents were Puerto Rican, but they accepted John and his family comfortably. Despite their poverty-stricken lives, their drug use and associated criminal activity, and their lack of education or any prospect of success in this competitive world, many of these men were admirable in their own way. John learned a great deal, but not enough, from these men. Pat and I may have learned more from John's experience in Hogar Crea. There is no question in my mind that these recovering addicts were better able to deal with drug addiction than the psychiatrists in John's prior rehabilitation environment.

After a period of recovery and subsequent relapse, John entered a rehab in Riverside, California, and a year later came back home to try one more time. Always we had an agreement that any drug use would send John back to Riverside. When after some promising months John did not return from his morning run, Pat and I confronted him when he got home after lunch. Yes, he had been using drugs, and yes, he knew that he would have to go back to California. Within an hour John was on a plane to Chicago on his way back to California. Everyone was in tears, but tough love requires standing by your rules.

Over the years of his struggles with addiction, John was typically clean and sober for several months and then in a period of crisis with drugs for several weeks, ending up again in treatment and continuing the cycle. Often the crises ended with a call home for help. One such call came from John in a pay phone in Riverside, California, asking me to direct the Riverside police to save him from the people who were trying to kill him. Knowing that any drug addict on the streets was necessarily involved with dangerous people, we didn't dismiss John's claim that his life was in danger. Drug dealers use addicts to transport both drugs and money to minimize their risk with the police, and John was entirely capable of stealing either valuable to feed his addiction, knowing that the dealer had to use fear to enforce the discipline of his transporters. As we spoke, however, we realized that John was delusional. He could see the police station across the intersection from his phone booth, but he was afraid to open the door and race across the street to safety. He wanted me to call the police and have them go get him. After some serious talking, John was persuaded to run to the police himself, and a kind officer escorted him to a nearby hospital. This was our first encounter with full-blown paranoia.

When John came home again in the next cycle of recovery, he was drug free for months and still bizarre in his behavior. When we finally took him to a psychiatrist for another opinion, that good man came out of his office after a half hour with John and announced that John was exhibiting the behavior of a schizophrenic. (Maybe this is what the psychologist saw so many years earlier that left him puzzled?) When the psychiatrist learned from us that John began using alcohol and other drugs at seventeen after a healthy and loving childhood, he explained that for male subjects with hereditary tendencies schizophrenia manifests itself at about seventeen, and very frequently the confused subject finds that alcohol is an effective self-medication. John's glass of wine at the television set was typical of such reactions. His tendency during his high school years to sit quietly in the darkness of the basement was further evidence that John was trying to block out the sensory stimuli that create confusion and sometimes fear for many schizophrenics. The great mystery of John's behavior was explained, but only after years of misdirected treatment. Only in his late twenties did we discover that John's drug addiction was compounded and probably initially stimulated by his schizophrenia. John had become a dual-diagnosis patient, a sufficiently common category to warrant books on the subject. Now we had two problems to solve simultaneously.

Any serious discussion of addiction to alcohol or other drugs must first acknowledge the seriousness of this affliction and the extreme difficulty of overcoming such a pernicious chronic illness. It would be wrong, however, to end in despair. Although programs for recovery fail to achieve permanent success more often than they succeed, it is important to the prospects of recovery that the family and friends of the addict never abandon their love and never give up the hope for recovery that keeps that possibility alive until death intervenes.

Pat and I never gave up on our kids, even as addictions early in their adult lives made it easier to just walk away. Tough love is sometimes the necessary alternative to enabling the addictions of family members, but it is love nonetheless. Pat and I managed to preserve our loving relationships with three children who battled through alcohol and drug addiction as young adults. Two of the three fought their way to recovery. John died at thirty-three, still in the bosom of his family.

## Schizophrenia

The psychiatrist who diagnosed John's schizophrenia on the basis of his observations in the office wanted John hospitalized for further observation. John was by then an adult and not an obvious danger to himself or to others, so his commitment to the psychiatric ward of St. Luke's Hospital in Bethlehem was at his discretion. We knew that John would not easily agree to hospitalization, so we drove him to the hospital parking lot without his foreknowledge of our destination. Once there, John balked. He said he was afraid to leave the car. We were stymied until a wonderful nurse came out to the car to talk to John. Under her calming influence he agreed to voluntary commitment.

The medication administered in the hospital snapped John out of the confused state associated with schizophrenia within twenty-four hours. Pat and I felt that our son had returned to us, despite the side effects evident from the medication available in those days (Haldol). From the doctor's perspective, the reaction to the medication confirmed the schizophrenia diagnosis and demonstrated that John's illness was treatable.

John did not find this news so comforting, however. He did not want to be classified as mentally ill and in need of lifelong medication.

For Pat and me, John's schizophrenia diagnosis was the answer to the mystery of his bizarre behavior over several years of drug abuse and self-destruction. If only he had been diagnosed at seventeen or eighteen, his life might have followed a less painful course. The medical profession did not yet understand what aberrations of the brain were involved in schizophrenia, but there was empirical evidence that the symptoms could be suppressed with certain drugs. The brain malfunctions that were involved with drug addiction were even less well understood, and there was no documented medical treatment to turn to.

Because schizophrenia is medically treatable and drug addiction currently is not, parents might prefer schizophrenia to drug addiction in their children. On the other hand, schizophrenia is presently incurable and drug addiction offers the hope of sustained recovery, however unpredictably. Which curse should parents prefer for their children? The only certain answer is that either is preferable to both together.

For the patient, however, the preference is clear. John felt the stigma of a recognized mental illness more acutely than he felt the societal disapproval of his drug abuse. He had a hard time accepting his drug addiction as a permanent condition, but that was much easier for him than admitting that he was "crazy" and would always be so.

John described in detail the side effects of his medication, sometimes in lament and sometimes in good humor. He asked if we remembered the way the patients walked in the movie *One Flew Over the Cuckoo's Nest*. "That's called the Haldol shuffle" by the psychiatric patients in his hospital, John told us, conveying not only a vivid illustration of this side effect of that drug but revealing also a remarkable degree of self-awareness by the patients.

The dual-diagnosis patient is constantly dealing with a Catch-22; the solution to his schizophrenia is to use mind-altering drugs, and this is precisely what he must avoid as a drug addict. His best prospect for help with schizophrenia is his psychiatrist, but the doctor is of little or no value in dealing with addiction. His best friend in dealing with addiction is the recovering addict, but the men in a tough drug rehab like Hogan Crea absolutely forbid the use of mind-altering drugs, even as medication.

The schizophrenia diagnosis may have helped Pat and me as John's parents to realize that his drug use was driven initially by his self-medication, but that realization did not alter the pattern of John's drug use, which continued intermittently for fifteen years. As John explained to me during a lucid interval of proper medication and abstinence from street drugs, he was attracted to the forbidden drugs not by the desire to feel high but by the need to control pain.

One can easily get the impression from the media that schizophrenics are dangerous people who hear voices commanding them to do evil things beyond their control. There may be such people, but John was not one of them. When not properly medicated John was inclined to withdraw into himself and become extremely passive. Before the onset of his schizophrenia, John was a vigorous athlete in sports that were inherently violent and he was probably more active sexually than most boys his age. As a schizophrenic John was quiet, slow moving, and uninterested in sex. When he was on the streets and out of touch, he was in a dangerous environment, but our greatest fear was that John would curl up in a culvert somewhere and die of dehydration and starvation. That fear was not ill-founded.

One of several California rehabs John entered before his schizophrenia diagnosis was run by recovering Hispanic addicts motivated by religious convictions. Pat and I visited John there and we were grateful to the good people running that house. At some point they called our home in Pennsylvania and reported that John had stopped eating, drinking, and talking to others. I was not at home, and Pat took the call. She told them to pick him up and take him to the hospital emergency ward, knowing that he was too weak to resist. In the hospital John was fed intravenously to keep him alive, but when Pat called, the nurse told her that John was comatose and not responding to any stimuli. Pat insisted that the nurse put the phone to John's ear, and he cried when he heard his mother's voice. So he came home again.

The house rules were clear to all: If you use drugs you cannot live with your parents. As long as John stayed on his medications for schizophrenia, he was able to stay drug free. But when he decided that he didn't need to continue his therapy or he objected to the side effects of his medications and abandoned them, he was likely to accept a beer or two and soon slip down the dangerous path to crack cocaine or whatever he found available.

On one such relapse, in 1999 as I recall, John was on the streets of Riverside after leaving his rehab prematurely, lost to Pat and me for some months. One Saturday afternoon in the spring I received in Tucson a phone call from John, begging for help and promising to stay clean. I asked John where he could be found in Riverside, but he was unable to answer. "I don't know," he said. He told me that he was at a public pay phone on a utility pole in the middle of a block, but he was afraid to leave the phone to walk to the corner to read the street signs. He said he would wait for me.

I was on a plane within the hour, determined to find my son somewhere in Riverside. I landed at the airport in nearby Ontario, rented a car, and drove to Riverside. After wandering aimlessly for a time, I asked local police where the street people lived and walked among them looking for John. I searched through the night with no success, finally taking a room for a few hours. I had found a public phone on a utility pole and I planned to go back there by daylight.

The next morning was Easter Sunday and I had hopes for a miracle, but I was disappointed. John was not at the pole, nor anywhere to be found. I called Pat and we decided that I should take the return flight home that I had scheduled, giving up on my fruitless search. I drove back to the Ontario airport, returned the rental car, and proceeded to my gate, only to discover that California had switched to daylight saving time and my plane was already gone.

I was, after all, a university president, so I had a briefcase full of work to fill in the hours before the next flight to Tucson. While I was waiting at the airport, Pat called and reported excitedly that John was on the other phone to the family home, back at that same pay phone in Riverside. I rented another car and found John still hanging on to that phone, incoherent and barely able to stand, but grateful to be rescued. I helped him into the car and raced back to the airport, where I needed a wheelchair to get him to the gate. It is surprising to me now that he was accepted for the flight with no identification, dirty, heavily bearded, and muttering like a wild man. I got him back to Tucson and took him directly to University Medical Center, where he responded to treatment very well.

Safely back on his medication for schizophrenia, John showed remarkable resilience, bouncing back to nearly normal. He completed two courses successfully at Pima Community College, moved into his own apartment, and began the journey to a new life.

In the late spring of 2002 John reported that the psychiatrist he was then seeing had agreed to reduce his medication dosage, which gave us pause. It was not long before Pat's eagle eye detected changes in John's behavior. He was sliding out of control again.

*With Wings as Eagles*

*John Likins*

OCTOBER 5, 1968 - JULY 19, 2002

⌁ *John's memorial
program (2002).
(Courtesy Beryl Martin
for Carillo Tucson
Mortuary program.)*

On July 19, 2002, John died in his bed, his system taxed beyond capacity by an unpredictably lethal mixture of prescription medicine and street drugs. He was thirty-three years old.

It is impossible to describe the grief of a parent confronting the death of a child of any age, except to others who have faced that loss. It seems contrary to the laws of nature, and therefore unreal. Pat and I needed immediately to see his still body, drained of all the energy that had created around him a special aura. We had to touch his once-powerful hands and kiss his cold forehead before his death was real to us.

At his memorial service, Pat and I both spoke about our son, singing his praises and lamenting the tragedy of his fall from a life of such vitality and promise. We asked for greater understanding of mental illness, whether it had a medical name like schizophrenia or a common name like drug addiction. We expressed the hope and the belief that collaborative research by physicians and neuroscientists will someday deepen our understanding of the malfunctions of the brain and lead to improved treatment of many forms of mental illness. Until that day comes, we prayed for compassion for our son.

## Principles

We all have principles and we live by them, more or less, most of the time. Only "other" people are "unprincipled." Most of us don't often actually examine our principles, so if we bend them a little or forget now and then, we suffer no pain. If our children are watching, however, or if we just imagine that our children know when we are compromising our principles, we are much more careful to be true to ourselves, to practice what we preach.

My children helped me to meet more than one challenge to my internal commitment to resist any pressure to treat anyone unfairly because of race, ethnicity, religion, gender, or sexual orientation. As the following example reveals, this was not always an easy commitment to uphold.

In late 1995 I appointed a search committee to find candidates qualified to serve Lehigh as dean of admissions and financial aid, naming two Lehigh trustees to that committee in addition to perhaps six others drawn from the campus community. The committee identified two unranked finalists and met with me to offer their counsel.

At this stage of a search process I want more from the committee members than just their votes; I want to hear an assessment of all surviving candidates from each individual member as we go around the table. This was not a stressful process in this instance; all committee members explicitly approved both candidates, some leaning one way and some leaning the other way. I was free to decide.

Both candidates were attractive young women with outgoing personalities and good background qualifications, but the older of the two candidates had directly relevant experience as an associate dean of admissions at Dartmouth and the other candidate had no admissions experience. On balance, I preferred the candidate from Dartmouth, but protocol required no announcement of my choice to the committee so I closed the meeting and ushered my guests out of my office without declaring my decision.

To my surprise, one trustee remained seated at my table. I knew that he would become chairman of the board in the coming July, a leadership choice I had encouraged among fellow trustees because he shared my vision for Lehigh and I liked the guy. I didn't know what to expect when he motioned me to return to my seat at the table.

"You know what you have to do," he said.

I must have responded with a blank stare.

My soon-to-be boss went on to say, "Lehigh is not ready for a black dean of admissions."

Lorna Hunter, the candidate from Dartmouth, is a black woman, and she was my choice. As chief executive officer of the university, I was formally authorized to make this decision, but as presumptive chairman of a large and relatively compliant board my dissenting trustee held my future in his capable hands. I hesitated and tried to keep my responses noncommittal; I did not challenge the man.

I agonized over this decision, which I recognized as a serious test of my commitment to my deeply held principles. Was I really willing to put my precious presidency on the line?

Although the five-year term of the gentleman then serving as chairman of the board was about to expire, I turned to him for help. He understood that I could not accept the instructions I had received from the board's chairman-elect, and he believed that, irrespective of trustee preferences for dean of admissions, the president's prerogative in making this decision should not be overridden by his board. He called a meeting of the board's executive committee, which unanimously voted to back their president (with the chairman-elect absent).

I won the battle, and more importantly Lorna proved her worth in the following year with an excellent strategic plan that was subsequently well executed. Even the new chairman of the board of trustees publicly applauded her performance.

As that new chairman began his five-year term, he told me that finding my successor would be his greatest responsibility. We seemed to be working harmoniously, but after one year together he let me know as I approached age sixty that he expected me to retire in two years.

University presidencies at this level are not jobs for which one applies; typically university representatives come to you to explore your interest in candidacy. During my Lehigh years I had turned aside several overtures from fine universities. (I declined to be a candidate for chancellor at UC Berkeley twice in one search, the second time knowing that despite my demurral I was one of five finalists.) At age sixty, however, I was unsure that such opportunities would continue to come my way.

Life has a way of turning out for the best if you just steer an honest course without sacrificing the principles you hold most dear. Without actively seeking a new position, I was blessed with an opportunity to move into a more prominent and more demanding presidency at the University of Arizona. When I was contacted about my interest in this assignment in Tucson, where Pat truly wanted to live, I competed successfully for the job, and ultimately served there for nine years, retiring at seventy. I left Lehigh in the fall of 1997, one year ahead of my chairman's schedule. He had pointed me to the door, but I left on my own terms for a better opportunity, principles intact. I knew that my children would be proud of me.

## Breaking Barriers

I accepted the University of Arizona presidency in July 1997 and moved our household to Tucson that summer, but I deferred my Arizona employment until October of that year so I could take proper care of unfinished business at Lehigh. We were in the final stages of creating the Zoellner Arts Center, a project the trustees had agreed to build on the basis of my assurance that Bob and Vickie Zoellner would actually cover all costs, although there was no written agreement to bind them to their expressed intentions. This was a transformational project for Lehigh and it was based entirely on trust. I stayed in the Lehigh presidency until the deal was consummated and attended the grand opening.

During this transition period, when my family had moved to Tucson but I was back at Lehigh to open the fall semester, I was jogging in the rain one morning when I came upon a long line of honking cars trying to gain entrance to the new parking structure near the Zoellner Center. The first car in that queue was occupied by a very frustrated woman who had properly inserted a paper pass into the new machine controlling the barrier to the entrance and found that the wet paper had jammed the mechanism. The line of cars behind her prevented her from backing out, and she had a class to teach in just a few minutes. She was stuck.

From her perspective, a stranger jogging by stopped to help. His cellphone call to the campus police didn't go through and he could not free the mechanism that would lift the nearly ten-foot-long wooden barrier on its hinges. So to her surprise he broke the board at its base! (It was only a one-inch by four-inch wooden board painted with black and white stripes.) The grateful motorist drove her car into the garage and rushed to class while I remained at the gate, collecting two-dollar parking fees from the other cars in the queue, until I was able to reach the campus police and get them to the scene.

When a month later my Lehigh friends bade me farewell as I made my final departure from campus, I received many mementos of my Lehigh presidency. Prominent among those gifts was the broken board from the parking structure barrier I had destroyed, suitably inscribed with the names of many Lehigh friends who saw this final act as symbolic of my legacy: Pete Likins broke barriers at Lehigh.

# 7

# Arizona . . . Home at Last

## Tucson

Pat was always eager for the challenges of new adventures in new locales until she moved to Tucson. After encouraging the moves from UCLA to Columbia, Columbia to Lehigh, and Lehigh to Arizona, she staked out her permanent home in Tucson, Arizona.

"You may go where you wish," she told me, "but I am staying here." I didn't have to be persuaded. I felt the same way.

After growing up together in beautiful Santa Cruz, California, and living for fourteen years in Southern California and for a total of twenty-two years in the East Coast cultures of Boston, New York/New Jersey, and eastern Pennsylvania, Pat and I found our true and natural home in Tucson, Arizona.

Tucson is a fascinating combination of the old and the new. Sometimes referred to as "the Old Pueblo," Tucson does preserve the feeling of an early Mexican town established on a riverbank where Indians had lived out their lives and cultivated their crops for thousands of years. At the same time, Tucson is a rapidly growing American city dominating a county of a million people, the vast majority of whom were born elsewhere, so being new to town does not take you out of the action.

Tucson is located in that southerly swath of Arizona that belonged to Mexico until 1854, when it was acquired through the transaction our schoolbooks call the Gadsden Purchase (although to Mexico it may have seemed more like extortion). Some prominent Mexican American families in Southern Arizona insist that their forebears did not cross the border into the United States; the border shifted to include their families. Tucson's history has been influenced significantly by generations of well-educated, wealthy, and powerful Mexican Americans, who in this unusual American town are not always assumed to be among the struggling masses near the bottom of the social order. The socioeconomic mix in Tucson is unusual and this changes the culture.

Tucson is the most comfortably diverse community in our experience, a place in harmony with the values most deeply held in our family. The urban cultures of Boston, New York, and Los Angeles are also quite diverse, but it sometimes feels that sharp lines separate people into categories in those environments. Either you are black or you are not black, either Mexican (as Mexican Americans are sometimes called) or American (a term sometimes reserved for Anglo Americans). Pat and I cannot live comfortably in environments that demand the division of the population into fixed categories, denying a proper identity to the millions of Americans who live on the blurry lines that artificially divide us. Where do our children fit into a society subdivided into racial and ethnic islands unconnected by the human bridges formed by families like mine?

Our son John always laughed about the labels strangers wanted to apply to him. In Pennsylvania he was usually assumed to be a Puerto Rican until he attempted to speak Spanish. On the urban streets of California after 9/11, his wild hair and bushy black beard made some people fear him as a deranged Arab. John was quite comfortable with Puerto Ricans, Arabs, and everyone else in the American spectrum, so he was more amused than offended, but he realized with some discomfort that he was not easily placed in an America with a compulsion for classification.

In Tucson it doesn't seem to matter how you might be classified by others. People are generally freed of the artificialities of formality or protocol. Most folks dress as they wish, speak up with straight talk when they want to be heard, and associate freely in any setting with friends and lovers in different racial or ethnic categories. Nobody seems to want to make a fuss just because you choose to be different. Pat and I realize that, although we look "normal," we are actually rather unconventional in our thinking. In Tucson that really is okay. We can be ourselves here and not feel out of place.

I was in a very visible and quite prominent position as the university president in a university town, but I didn't experience the isolation that frequently accompanies such prominence. I was often approached by strangers in a restaurant or a bank or a supermarket just to exchange a word or two about the Wildcats or the latest dustup with the state legislature. Not only alumni but ordinary citizens of Tucson have stopped me just to express their thanks for my work on behalf of the university or the football program or the Hispanic students or some other aspect of the university they cared about. Students on campus were similarly friendly and familiar with their president—the same students who more often at Lehigh would have been more reserved, at Columbia more aggressive, and at UCLA simply indifferent. I have always enjoyed connecting with people at every level without the obstacles (or the pretensions) of high office. In the Southern Arizona environment these connections are quite natural.

For all these reasons, Tucson is a relatively welcoming environment for people who don't quite fit in with the mainstream of American society, for people of color or different religions or sexual orientation, and for women. (These people are collectively a majority of our population in America, but they don't often define the dominant culture.)

In subtle ways, Pat felt more respected and more personally welcomed in Tucson than anywhere else we had lived. Protocol in New York City put me on the stage at grand affairs and my wife at a table in the audience; in Tucson we sit at a table together and she is welcomed at the microphone. At Lehigh she was told that as the president's wife she was expected to put the university first and family second; in Tucson family always comes first.

During the decade and more that we have lived in Tucson, the governor of the state of Arizona has always been a woman, with Republican Jane Hull succeeded by Democrat Janet Napolitano followed by Republican Jan Brewer. For most of that time my congressman was an openly gay man (Republican); now a woman (Democrat) holds that high office. Despite the well-deserved reputation of the Arizona legislature as being dominated by benighted archconservatives, the people of Arizona, and especially the people of Tucson, are generally quite open-minded and warm-hearted.

I don't want to seem naive in praising the Tucson culture; the legacies of a racist history still linger in some situations and rabid politicians can still stir up latent fears among the people. Relatively speaking, however, Tucson is a comfortably diverse environment.

Many of Tucson's residents are drawn to this area of the country by the abundant sunshine and the beautifully stark desert mountains. Pat and I love it here because of the people.

~ Pete with
Arizona cheer-
leaders (c. 1998).
(University of
Arizona photo.)

## University of Arizona

Thousands of students and football fans first saw their new president personally in 1997 on the football field with an Arizona cheerleader standing on his shoulders to lead the crowd's cheers. (I first pulled this stunt spontaneously at Lehigh in 1984 with a student on my shoulders named Bobby Weaver, an Olympic champion wrestler, and I did it every year thereafter with cheerleaders for more than twenty years.)

In a more formal setting that fall, I greeted the assembly at my presidential inauguration ceremonies without preamble as follows:

"Hang on, folks. We're going to take a little ride together, and I see white water ahead."

At my first Arizona commencement, in December 1997, I told the story of the wooden barrier to the new parking structure at Lehigh that I had broken to admit a frustrated teacher stuck at the front of a queue of honking cars. More importantly, I told the following sequel to that story.

When the teacher was liberated at the entrance to the parking structure by a man she saw as a stranger, she rushed to her class, which was a summer bridge class designed for disadvantaged students (mostly minorities) to help them prepare for the freshman class experience at Lehigh. She arrived in class a bit late and told her students about the man who broke the barrier to her admission. The class spontaneously broke into applause!

Upon reflection, the teacher found an explanation for this unexpected applause in the resonance these new Lehigh freshmen felt with the stranger in the story. They, too, were breaking barriers just by enrolling at Lehigh University, and the stranger's actions put them in good company. Neither the students nor the teacher knew at the time that their own personal Good Samaritan was the Lehigh president, but when they uncovered his identity they felt even more strongly that barriers could be broken at Lehigh.

The grateful teacher wrote me a letter after I made my move to Arizona. I read from this letter in my December commencement address, dramatically lifting over my head the nearly ten-foot board that had been a barrier at Lehigh.

I sent a clear message to those attending my first Arizona commencement: Barriers to learning will not be tolerated at this university.

In my first few months in Arizona I was trying to establish real action agenda, trying to say to all who would listen: "We're going to take a good place and make it better!"

When I began my Lehigh presidency, I was not quite forty-six and conscious of my need for a deeper understanding of my mission; I openly devoted my first year to the education of the president. When I began my Arizona presidency fifteen years later, at age sixty-one, I felt a new sense of urgency. By that time I knew what I wanted to do with the rest of my life, so I stepped up the pace and pushed a little harder. I knew that I could open up opportunities for everybody, not just for people like me. I knew that the very best place to do this was in a very fine research university. I saw my job as advancing two agenda that many would see as disparate: (1) Accelerate the rapid rise of the University of Arizona as a nationally prominent research university. (2) Develop and refine the culture of the University of Arizona as a nurturing environment where all kinds of capable people could achieve their full potential. Although the second of these objectives was surely not perceived by most observers as a major element of my life as a busy president who must first manage the crises of the day and only then pursue the longer-term agenda, in this book it is the second cause above that must receive the emphasis.

The University of Arizona was perhaps the perfect place for me to pursue these two agenda simultaneously. Largely through the creative efforts of superb professors who found in this university the kind of open and unstructured academic environment that encourages interdisciplinary research, the University of Arizona was becoming one of the top research universities in America. UA research funding as reported by the National Science Foundation reached the highest level in the nation in the physical sciences in 2005 and again in 2008. In 2006, as I retired from the presidency, the UA was second in the physical sciences and thirteenth overall among public universities. Despite the absence of the kind of enlightened public investment that was so visible in competing state universities, such as the University of California, the academic performance of the UA faculty is truly world-class. And yet the population on campus is remarkably diverse for a research university. It really is possible to make good progress on both agenda, achieving intellectual excellence with human diversity.

The University of Arizona is unlike any other university in my experience. The student body is unusually diverse for a major research university, in terms of race, ethnicity, national origin, religion, and socio-economic status. The faculty as a whole is intellectually powerful, unusually creative, and extremely successful in the national competition for the research funds that drive the university at its core. Faculty move more easily across disciplines in this university than I have observed elsewhere, resulting in worldwide leadership in such cross-disciplinary fields as optical sciences, astronomy and space sciences, anthropology, and a wide variety of studies relating to water, from hydrogeology to water law. Research contracts won by faculty in fierce national competition bring in more money than the sum of allocations of taxpayer dollars by the state and payment of tuition dollars (net of financial aid) by Arizona residents. Under these circumstances, it would be very easy to develop a culture in which the commitment to students and outreach to the community were overwhelmed by the need to compete effectively for research dollars, but I found many members of the Arizona faculty, even those with the best research credentials, deeply committed to their mission of education and service to the community. Never have I seen so many professors reach so high for the stars in the research firmament and at the same time reach down so graciously into an undergraduate student body that is so wide-ranging in its preparation for studies in a top-flight university. Most faculty members accept not only a responsibility to their students but a duty to their community, both for economic development and for enriching the culture.

The key to gaining acceptance of diversity as a worthy objective in recruiting students and faculty in a serious research university is perceiving diversity as an element of quality, not a special consideration apart from quality, which is always the proper selection criterion.

Among the most important attributes in an old white guy who wants to advance the diversity agenda is humility. If you don't recognize what you don't know and perhaps can't know, you cannot achieve what your heart desires. Some of my most important learning experiences over the years came from individual students, faculty, and staff on campus, but I also learned a great deal from members of the Tucson community. To tap into this resource, I established six community advisory councils to represent different sectors of the community: Hispanics, Native Americans, African Americans, Asian Americans, the disabled, and the lesbian-gay-bisexual-transgender (LGBT) coalition. All six groups met regularly, often with me and other officers of the university in attendance. There is very little hostility to any of these groups in Tucson or on the University of Arizona campus, but there is a surfeit of ignorance and a common distrust. These six community advisory councils were very helpful in reducing my own ignorance and dispelling the community's distrust of the University of Arizona.

The greatest challenge to the culture of tolerance at the University of Arizona in my time was in the aftermath of the terrorist attacks of 9/11. We knew immediately after the airliners brought down the World Trade Center towers in New York that in Tucson our concern should focus not on terrorists but on the danger of misplaced rage manifesting itself as retribution wreaked upon innocent people of the Muslim faith or from Middle Eastern countries. We held a public assembly on the campus mall by noon on that fateful day, and the following day there were joint Jewish/Muslim prayer services on the mall as well as Christian services, all in an attempt to keep anger properly focused and keep fear under control. I met in my office and at the local mosque with frightened Muslim or Middle Eastern students, some of them from other countries and others who were born in America of immigrant parents. After a turbaned Sikh (not a Muslim) was shot to death in Phoenix by a passing motorist, I discovered a small community of Sikhs in our student body, concerned for their safety. (After centuries of Sikh conflict with Muslims in India, they found themselves in danger of being attacked as Muslims in America!) This was a dangerous time, a true test of the ability of the University of Arizona and Tucson communities to look past the terrorist provocations to accept on their individual merits the members of our communities who had suddenly become very vulnerable minorities. There were some awkward moments, but no violence on campus or in Tucson. We passed a very severe test and I was proud of our people.

The struggle for civil rights in America has often been met with violence, with race riots on a large scale still not matching the virulence of the recurring incidents of hangings and bombing and burning throughout our history. We are now in a better time, when any such behavior is almost universally condemned, but we still carry memories of this past and its consequences for those now living in America. We have honest disagreements in the twenty-first century about the justification of affirmative action to rectify some of the injustices of the past. In my experience it is not fruitful to focus on the past in the advocacy of affirmative action; there is abundant justification in the present. America needs the talents and efforts of its entire population, which is increasingly diverse.

The dominant ethos of the state of Arizona has been to provide the illusion of accessibility to the state's three public universities by keeping tuition and admissions standards uniformly very low. By the policies of the Arizona Board of Regents, when I arrived in 1997 graduates of Arizona's high schools in the top half of their classes meeting certain course requirements were assured of admission to any of Arizona's three public universities and they paid the lowest tuition among public flagship universities in America. However, we had almost no financial aid from the state to offer our most impoverished students, and without financial aid many Arizona citizens could not afford to send their children to our universities, even with very low tuition. Once admitted, many graduates of Arizona high schools found themselves unprepared academically and intimidated socially in the environment of the University of Arizona, while still obliged to work part time to cover their costs, even with low tuition. The result was a high dropout rate in comparison with our nation's best public research universities, all of which had higher entrance requirements and better financial aid for needy students. As much as I admired the University of Arizona even as I arrived, I realized that there was work to be done in easing the external constraints that kept this fine university from achieving its full potential, both as an academic institution and as a supportive environment for promising students, even those who had historically found all research universities beyond their reach.

By the time I retired in 2006, the University of Arizona was obliged by the board of regents to admit only those course-qualified Arizona high school graduates in the top quarter of their classes, with individual university discretion to admit selectively from students in the second quartile. Tuition was still low, but no longer at the bottom, remaining near the top of the bottom third nationally. Financial aid was much more well budgeted (at the cost of tuition revenues), so our university was actually more affordable for the very poor than it had been when tuition was much lower. Students of color were enrolling in increasing numbers and improving their graduation rates. We were rapidly changing the culture and slowly getting better in fact. We stretched the fabric and it did not tear.

## Intercollegiate Athletics

I know from my own experience at Stanford how profoundly athletic competition can shape one's sense of self. I know from decades of working with coaches and student athletes during my years at Columbia, Lehigh, and Arizona that athletic competition can give young men and women critical developmental experiences not otherwise available to them. I have personal knowledge of the experiences of individual student athletes whose entire lives unfolded differently for them because they were able to prove themselves in the arena. Two such stories stand out for their unexpected outcomes.

Richie Owens was a Lehigh football recruit from inner-city Philadelphia who nearly flunked out after his freshman year. He had been a good student without effort in high school, and until he was living with other football players off campus at Lehigh he had no idea how to study. Once he realized that schoolwork required the same kind of disciplined effort that football practice required, it was very nearly too late. He knew he would lose his scholarship unless he completed two courses over the summer with grades of B or better, and he had no way to pay summer-school tuition.

When a faculty friend, Dr. Patti Ota, brought Richie to see me in the President's Office, I could see that he was desperate to stay at Lehigh, which he knew was his ticket out of the neighborhood in Philly. He knew, too, that he would gravely disappoint his mama if he missed this opportunity, and I could see that, like many young black men of high promise, his mama was very important to him. I could also see that Richie was a very impressive young man, obviously intelligent and sincere in his appeal. However, I had to explain to this aspiring football player that I could not give him money for tuition without exceeding the maximum allowed by the NCAA, thereby destroying his eligibility for football. He was eager to make that sacrifice if it would enable him to stay at Lehigh and ultimately to graduate. I wrote Lehigh a personal check for $600 and Richie enrolled in two courses, earning B grades in both and restoring his scholarship. He remained at Lehigh in good standing, watching his former teammates from the sidelines.

In Richie's fourth year at Lehigh, on track to graduate after one more year, he came to see me with a new proposal. He had discovered that he would be eligible for one season of football if he repaid the $600, which he was then prepared to do. I accepted the unexpected money and Richie went back to the game that brought him to Lehigh in the first place. He broke his hand in preseason play, but even with his hand in a cast he had a pretty good year as a defensive end.

I would have been more than satisfied if this had been the end of the Richie Owens story. But in the spring before his Lehigh graduation Richie tried out for the National Football League and got drafted by the Washington Redskins. Despite his very limited experience in college football, and that in an NCAA Division IAA school, Richie's extraordinary talent earned him the opportunity he deserved. He quickly made the starting lineup, led the Redskins in quarterback sacks, and began what would become a long and productive career in professional football.

Richie came back to Lehigh more than once to express his gratitude, and he e-mailed me in Arizona a decade or more later to reiterate his thanks. Richie is a fine man with a good life that almost slipped away when he was eighteen. I put my faith in this promising young man at that critical time in his youth, and I was richly rewarded by his success.

Shauntinice Polk gave me another deeply rewarding experience with a student athlete, this time in Arizona. "Polky," as she was called, was a very promising women's basketball recruit at the University of Arizona, but her academic test scores and high school performance properly gave serious pause to the university's director of admissions. Although the director knew that I had never given instructions to admit any student at either Arizona or Lehigh, despite the occasional pressure from well-placed alumni and benefactors, she told the anxious basketball coach, Joan Bonvicini, that only the president could admit Ms. Polk. I agreed to interview her.

When Polky came into my office for her interview, we were both a bit intimidated. Polky was a foot taller than I am and about a hundred pounds heavier. Nonetheless, that day she was a frightened little girl. She was quiet, but she spoke well of her determination to learn, noting the presence at the UA of the excellent Strategic Alternative Learning Techniques (SALT) program for students with learning disabilities. It was too late for admission to the fall semester after her high school graduation, so she proposed to dedicate herself in the coming spring semester to her studies if she could only have a chance to prove herself.

I gave her that chance, insisting that basketball be set aside in her life and requiring that she periodically report her academic progress to me personally. She agreed to the terms and did as promised.

At the end of her first semester, Polky proudly entered the President's Office with her head held high. With tears in her eyes she reported her fine grades for the semester, gleefully declaring, "I can learn!" She spoke of her plans for graduation and eventually a career teaching students with learning disabilities. The SALT program had performed another miracle, she said, but I assured her that she deserved the credit herself. The SALT program instructors can show you how to do it, but they can't do it for you. (As further evidence of her success in getting her act together that semester, she had lost sixty pounds, getting ready for her future in basketball.)

Polky became a sensation, "the most popular athlete on campus," according to men's basketball coach Lute Olson. Her success on the basketball court was unmatched in the history of women's basketball at Arizona, but more than that she became a bold leader, not afraid to call out "Here comes the little guy!" when I visited the locker room after a big win.

Then one morning in Polky's senior year my President's Cabinet meeting was interrupted with the shocking news that Polky had just then suddenly passed out and died in the gym. I rushed from the meeting to be with the coaches and the players as they struggled to come to grips with reality. Their beloved Polky was dead, probably the victim of an errant blood clot traveling from an injured knee, but the cause didn't really matter. She was gone.

I shed tears over Polky's loss, as did countless others. I flew with the team to Hanford, California, where Polky had carried her team to state championships while living without family support, struggling to deal with the social pressures on a black girl of unusual dimensions even in early childhood, forging the personal strength that enabled her to overcome great obstacles in college. I participated in memorial services in Hanford and in Tucson, controlling my emotions with great difficulty. Polky's life is a tale of triumph over great adversities, but it ended too soon.

Richie Owens's story had a surprise ending, and so did Polky's. I put my faith in both of them, and made two good decisions in doing so.

As these stories illustrate, I believe that the importance of intercollegiate athletics lies in its potential for human development of young men and young women. Others may focus on the school spirit stimulated by successful teams in football or basketball, and still others might imagine a positive effect of such winning teams on recruiting or fund-raising, but I see these benefits as quite secondary (or even imaginary). The reason for continuing to sponsor intercollegiate athletics in American colleges and universities in a wide variety of sports is to provide unique learning experiences for students who are capable of the disciplined effort demanded by athletic competition at a high level of intensity.

In my experience, the value of the learning experience does increase with the pressure felt by the athlete and that depends on the level of intensity of the competition. I'm not persuaded that it depends on the level of skill demonstrated by the participating athletes; the Lehigh-Lafayette football game can be as intense as the Texas-Oklahoma game, with the pressure to win in that most-played American football rivalry felt as keenly as the warriors in Texas and Oklahoma feel that same pressure.

Although these learning opportunities were historically first made available to the young white males from "good families" who had the privilege of a college education in America, as society opened college doors more widely and pure athletic talent became more important to college recruiting, these opportunities for personal development were increasingly realized by people of color, and in certain high-visibility sports especially by African Americans. Some of the most powerful images defined by black Americans were at least initially associated with black athletes, but far more important are the thousands of American "minorities" who first defined their own self-worth in athletic competition and continued their pattern of success in business, law, education, politics, or wherever their talents enabled them to prosper.

There is a dark side to the influence of sports competition on the lives of young people of color, particularly for black athletes in sports that have the elusive potential for great riches. For every black football or basketball player who is ruined by success there must be a thousand youngsters who falsely imagine that their athletic skills promise such rewards that they can neglect other aspects of their development, including formal education. Even as I applaud the developmental benefits of athletic competition, I must advocate social policies nationally that minimize the risk of bad things happening to vulnerable young people.

I have made it my practice in university presidencies to talk candidly to assembled coaching staff, reminding them of their great responsibilities in developing aspects of their charges that have no obvious relationship to their game. I want them to know that I believe that in many cases they have more influence for good or ill on their young athletes than anyone else in the university because they reach them to their very souls in times of great vulnerability. I respect and admire the coaching profession at its best, but I have no regard for coaches who take advantage of their student athletes for their own gain, even if they win overwhelmingly.

I entered university life as a freshman at Stanford in 1953 and retired from the University of Arizona presidency in 2006. I witnessed very significant changes in university cultures over that long span of fifty-three years, especially as they relate to women and people of color. I'd like to think that I played some small role in advancing some of those changes. Among the most significant of these changes, in my opinion, was the dramatic expansion of opportunities for women to compete in athletics at a very high level. I expect to see a significant impact of women's sports on the development of leaders in our society, especially in business, politics, and such demanding professions as medicine and law.

I once served on a corporate board with a woman, herself a CEO, who told me unequivocally that she would not be in that role had she not played college basketball at the highest level. Such anecdotes are becoming increasingly commonplace.

It is not possible to succeed for very long in such competitive environments as business and politics without the qualities of self-discipline, perseverance, stamina, grace in combat, and resilience in occasional defeat that come with athletic competition. If you want to prepare yourself for such a life, intercollegiate athletics at the highest level is the best experience I can imagine. (If I had a little more imagination, or a different kind of personal history, I might see the life of a dancer at the highest level to be comparably valuable, and there must be other examples, but I can speak only from what I know.)

## Diversity

In the fall of 1997, early in my Arizona presidency, I was welcoming a group of National Merit scholars newly enrolled in the freshman class at a dinner in their honor. I addressed the assembly before dinner, and as dessert was being served I circulated among them, table-hopping to cover the half dozen or so tables in the dining room.

By chance I pulled up a chair next to a small blond woman in a wheelchair. The usual questions took an unexpected turn.

"What's your name?" I asked.

"Cheri Blauwet," said the freshman.

"Where are you from?"

"Iowa."

"What brings you from Iowa to the University of Arizona?"

"Wheelchair track."

"What?"

With a marked elevation of intensity, Cheri said, "Wheelchair track! Don't you know that you have one of the best wheelchair track teams in America?"

Properly chastised, I had to admit that I was still new and hadn't discovered that treasure, but I welcomed the opportunity to learn more.

Cheri made an appointment with her new friend the president and entered my office a week later with three classmates in wheelchairs and one who was blind, all student athletes in Arizona's excellent Adaptive Athletics program, which includes track, basketball, rugby, and goalball (for the blind). At Stanford I had competed with a blind wrestler, for whom the rules were adapted only by requiring constant contact, so I understood the concept of adaptive athletics. I was intrigued, and I learned enough in that one meeting to permanently alter my perception of what it means to be "disabled."

When years later I wrote a letter of recommendation for Cheri to Stanford's College of Medicine, where she subsequently completed her M.D. degree, I described her as one of the most able people I had ever met, despite the isolated disability that had confined her to a wheelchair since an accident at the age of two. She had completed her Arizona degree in molecular biology with nearly perfect grades and earned multiple medals in the Paralympics in both Sydney and Athens. Later she progressed from her successes in races at 50, 100, and 200 meters to the New York Marathon, always challenging for the gold. I told the Stanford College of Medicine admissions committee that beyond her intellectual powers, Cheri's buoyant personality and positive attitude would not only carry her through the rigors of Stanford's medical training but teach her fellow students important lessons in humility.

Cheri taught me those lessons too.

Until I moved to Tucson, already past my sixtieth year, I had not properly understood the full dimensions of the diversity issue, which had been framed in my mind in primarily racial terms. Spending a lifetime in a wheelchair will give anyone a different perspective than an able-bodied person of any race, and that perspective can be valuable for all of us to understand.

When I first came to Arizona I was surprised to hear the term "Native American" used interchangeably with the word "Indian," which I thought had been discarded in the evolution of a "politically correct" vocabulary. I asked a Native American legislator for guidance.

"Sally," I said, "what do you want to be called?"

"I am a Yaqui," she said proudly, naming her tribe. "Other labels don't matter to me."

Tribal identities are very real and tribal cultures are very different from one another, even in a given region of the country. The Hopi see the world through different eyes than the Navajo, even if they live side by side. The challenges that must be overcome by two Northern Arizona Indians from these two tribes in adapting to the Western culture of the University of Arizona are significantly different.

In American society we often lump together as "Asian Americans" people of vastly different ancestral heritage in such countries as India, China, Japan, Korea, and the Philippines, to name a few among many.

Muslims from Indonesia, the country with the largest Muslim population, see the world very differently than the Muslims of Saudi Arabia,
even if they all turn their eyes to Mecca for prayer. As we see every day
in our newspapers, even in a given country the major sects of the Muslim
faith have quite different perspectives. The same phenomenon is apparent
in both Christian and Jewish religions. The Sunni/Shiite divide in Iraq has
obvious parallels to the Protestant/Catholic conflict in Northern Ireland.
We can only hope that it can be as nearly resolved.

When we search for illustrations of diversity among the people we
know, we need look no farther than the span from our most politically
conservative relative to the most liberal. Even people who look alike
and grow up in similar environments can emerge as adults with polarized political beliefs. Acceptance of diversity is important even within a
single family.

Obviously the dimensions of human diversity are vast. When we
open our minds to the possibilities, we see limitless opportunities to
stretch our thinking and expand our perspectives. Many people decide
not to make this choice, but they can't deny the possibilities.

My own thinking about the importance of embracing diverse populations in America (and especially in American universities) has evolved in
the course of the past fifty years. In the 1960s, when Pat and I awakened
to the significance of the civil rights movement, we saw the conflicts
then wracking the country over race as a struggle for social justice. Our
motivations came from the heart and from our embrace of the ideals of
the American democracy. The drive for racial equality then came largely
from such social institutions as churches, schools, and many governmental
organizations, with active or passive resistance coming from society's tra-
ditionally economic institutions, such as corporations and labor unions,
and from social institutions in the southeastern American states. Only
those of us who were most idealistic and most passionate were optimistic
about winning the war underlying the battles for civil rights.

As I approached the end of my professional life in 2006, I realized
that my motivations had expanded to embrace a pragmatic concern that
America could not afford to rely for its economic future on the efforts
of straight, white, Christian males, who had always been a minority and
would increasingly be so in America. I realized that many of America's
economic institutions, from corporations to labor unions, had become
advocates of policies to advance opportunities for women and minorities,
while the federal government at that time and various state governments

had become sources of active or passive resistance. I observed changing attitudes in America's southern states as they developed greater economic strength. As the rationale for diversity had expanded from concern for the oppressed to concern for America, the tide had turned. Now there is every reason to believe that Americans will pull together to enable our country to draw upon the creative talents and the energies of all of its people, not just straight, white, Christian males.

America's colleges and universities have always been arenas in which advocates for social change have thrived, but in the 1960s there was considerable tension between the institutions and their people, between their administrations on the one hand and their students and faculty on the other (although relationships were never as polarized as they appeared in the media). In the twenty-first century it has become apparent that no college or university can prosper for very long if it fails to include in its populations men and women of significant diversity, if only because students learn so much informally from the people with whom they interact on campus. To fail to provide students with a diverse human environment is to fail to provide them with the education they will need for the global environment in which they will compete after graduation. The needed diversity is not limited to race and ethnicity. Students must learn from every available source and develop the intellectual sophistication needed to sort out points of view that are compatible with their own mission in life and their own moral values.

The evolution of my thinking about the "big picture" of diversity in America paralleled the expansion of my personal understanding of the complexities of life for our children. Pat and I had adopted our racially diverse children because we wanted a beautiful family and not because we were trying to change the world. In our society at that time, and still today, there are many more children of color who need a family than there are blue-eyed blonds. We understood the implications of that reality, but we did not immediately accept the obligation to try to change it. Inevitably, however, our experiences with our children opened our eyes and enabled us to see the sometimes subtle slights that people of color live with all the time. We better understood the impatience for progress that black parents were feeling, knowing that society cannot change fast enough to spare their children from pain. We better understood why people of color must wonder, when things go wrong in their lives, if racial prejudice was a factor; we recognized that the wondering itself can become a source of tension between the races. We began to accept our responsibilities.

As my professional opportunities developed, and I found myself in first one and then another university presidency over a span of twenty-four years, I became increasingly conscious of my responsibility to lend my growing strength to the cause of advancing the diversity agenda in America. When I arrived at Lehigh for my first presidency, I imagined that the example of my family would speak adequately for my beliefs, but in time I began to feel that this was no substitute for active personal engagement. In retrospect I believe that my most important efforts in this arena at Lehigh focused on developing personal relationships with Lehigh's small minority student populations, trying to make them feel that they were in a supportive environment where they could realize their full potential. We reasoned that only if currently enrolled students were happy with Lehigh could we expect future students with the same cultural affinities to commit to a Lehigh education, so we built confidence in Lehigh from the ground up. This was a challenge at Lehigh because of the history and traditions of the place. It was much easier at the University of Arizona.

The biggest obstacle to progress on the diversity front at the University of Arizona was the hovering presence of state legislators with real budgetary power seeking to impose their own social agenda on students. In my very first testimony before the state's House Appropriations Committee, my first question came from a legislator who wanted to know how I planned to remove pornography from the Internet. I got the impression that my university budget depended upon my answer, but I had no way to control the Internet. We were continually bombarded with attacks on such "radical" academic programs as Women's Studies and Africana Studies. We listened during budget hearings to allegations that we were wasting taxpayer money by educating illegal immigrants and their children. Politicians in power wanted to be assured that we were not acting affirmatively to increase minority enrollments, while politicians out of power wanted the opposite assurances. We followed the Supreme Court cases carefully and acted accordingly.

One of the toughest issues of our time deals with the lingering prejudice against gays and lesbians. Religious organizations, including my own Catholic Church, legitimize this bias for many people. Just as the Catholic Church had difficulty accepting the realities of the physical universe in the time of Galileo, the realities of the biological universe are being denied in our own times. The result is the apparent countenancing of ignorant and inhumane behavior by many believers in the love of Jesus.

The official manifestation of institutional bias focuses on same-sex domestic partners. Should they be permitted to marry or otherwise commit to authorized civil unions? Should they have spousal access to partners in critical hospital care? Should they enjoy health-care benefits or other benefits given to spouses of public employees?

Although the domestic partners of public university employees were enjoying spousal benefits in all PAC 10 universities except those in Arizona when I arrived in Tucson, and this was the national pattern for the universities with which we competed for faculty, as president of the University of Arizona I had no authority to grant such benefits. The one domestic-partner benefit under control by the three university presidents was the modest tuition benefit extended to the spouses and children of university employees.

With the encouragement of President Gary Stuart of the Arizona Board of Regents, President Michael Crow of Arizona State University (ASU) and I agreed one summer that we would extend our tuition benefit plans to domestic partnerships for same-sex couples in Arizona, where they were not permitted to marry. We worked on this plan for an entire year, consulting with regents and representatives of the gay and lesbian communities on our campuses, coordinating our programs carefully in the knowledge that our political vulnerabilities in the legislature would be ameliorated if we acted in concert.

When the day came for our joint announcement, ASU was silent. President Crow had changed his mind, although he didn't tell us that in advance. The University of Arizona went forward as promised, feeling vulnerable to budgetary punishment by the legislature.

Michael justified his inaction with the following explanation: "Pete, you are a relationship-based manager and I am a fact-based manager. If the facts change, or my perception of the facts changes, my decision can change. You are constrained by your need to consider the impact of your actions on other people. That's why I can change my positions rapidly when you cannot."

Michael is an astute politician and a very successful president at Arizona State University. I think he knew himself and he knew me as well. It didn't seem to bother him that his explanation left no room for trust.

Remember Dr. Seuss? What would I do if I ran the zoo? It turns out that constraints both external and internal keep the zookeeper in check.

A university president can encourage the decision-makers in admissions and financial aid to bring in a diverse freshman class, but the president does not normally select individual freshmen. The president can encourage faculty search committees to see diversity as an element of quality and not a separate matter, but the president does not unilaterally choose new faculty members. The president does decide who will be the vice presidents of the university and who will serve on the President's Cabinet.

At the University of Arizona I was able to create genuine diversity on my leadership team. At one point when the cabinet had twenty members, ten were men and ten were women. Even when I reduced the size of the cabinet I was able to preserve its diversity. At various times four Hispanics served in my cabinet. Two African Americans were in the cabinet as I concluded my service, including the new president of the University of Arizona Foundation. At one point, nine cabinet members were vice presidents, including one white male, one Hispanic male, and seven women, one black and one Hispanic. The provost and executive vice president was a white male and the two senior vice presidents were a Hispanic male and a black female. This group of campus leaders was as diverse as any that could be found among the nation's research universities.

## Courage

As I was driving north on U.S. 101 in 1960, with Pat lying down with her Siamese cat in the backseat and her brother Bee by my side, my Opel sedan and the car ahead were passed by a big diesel rig, a truck tractor with no trailer. As the two-lane road curved, the truck blocked the southbound lane and an oncoming little Renault Dauphine sedan had nowhere to go but the depression on the west side of the road.

Bee and I watched the accident unfold a hundred yards ahead, and then we froze as the Dauphine fishtailed, rolled, and then tumbled end over end down the highway, landing on the hood of our car, bursting into flames, and bouncing over our heads to land behind us in the depression on the east side of the road.

Bee got out of the car groggily, dazed by breaking the windshield with his head, and I, unhurt, helped Pat from the backseat. Cars were stopping all around us on that busy highway, and everyone saw the flaming little Dauphine on the roadside nearby as a gasoline bomb about to explode. We started to run.

To my amazement, I saw the passenger door opening on the Dauphine, which was resting on its wheels after all that bouncing around.

Someone was alive in there, despite the violent tumbling and the raging flames. I checked my impulse to run and made my way down the slope to the burning car. The driver was unconscious, but her passenger was struggling to save her friend. I got them both out of the car and up the slope to the highway, driven by adrenaline and not thinking at all. In my blind instinct I saved the lives of two young women, who as it turned out were California schoolteachers bound for home in Wisconsin. After it was all over and I had time to think, I was proud of passing one of life's important tests. You don't really know what you would do in such a situation until the moment comes.

Pat held on to her cat despite cracked vertebrae in her neck, Bee got a nasty bump on the head, and I was slightly toasted from the fire. The schoolteachers survived, probably with plastic surgery for the badly burned driver. Both cars were totally destroyed, but everyone lived to tell the tale.

Is this a test of courage? What does that word mean?

Although the etymology of the word "courage" suggests passion of the heart, its necessary elements are risk to oneself and dedication to other people or principles. Risking one's life to save the lives of others, as above, illustrates the idea dramatically, but this may not be the highest level of courage. It may take greater courage to defend a principle under fire than it takes to save a life, if only because of the time available for reflecting upon the risks. Saving lives usually requires instantaneous action taken so spontaneously that it may better be characterized symbolically as coming from the heart than coming from the mind. Risking a career for a principle is a more deliberate and considered act, driven by a passion of the heart but informed by a rational awareness of risks and consequences.

I passed the test of courage on the highway, but I take more pride in passing the test at Lehigh, defying the explicit instructions of the chairman-elect not to engage a black woman, Lorna Hunter, as dean of admissions and financial aid. I had time to think that over and still did the right thing.

Before I throw out my shoulder patting myself on the back, I should pause to think about the courage required of Lorna Hunter, who accepted the Lehigh challenge as dean of admissions and financial aid knowing that the chairman of the board had tried to block her appointment. I marveled at her poise when she presented a creative recruitment plan to the board of trustees during her first year, overcoming her fears and earning the respect of the board, including the chairman. That must have been a particularly challenging time for her, but she had to be brave every day of her life just to survive. That takes a special kind of courage, much greater than was demanded of me.

Pat has that kind of courage. The spotlight was not focused on her as it was on me, but in many ways she is the more courageous. She didn't falter when a doctor told her to reject for adoption the infant with a congenital heart defect. She didn't hesitate to adopt a black child who needed a family, or a second black child, or a Mexican American child, or two Indian children who brought with them the scars of seven to ten years of difficult and chaotic life. In every one of these instances, and in many more, Pat was the courageous initiator and I followed her lead, fully supportive but not the primary force.

Courage is a quality highly valued in our American culture. We won't elect a politician who sacrifices people and principles to save himself or herself at the polls, and we may admire political courage even when we disagree with the values loyally defended. We don't respect the colleague who dissembles to avoid the consequences of his or her actions, and we value the man or woman who faces squarely the responsibility for mistakes made. We see courage as a more elemental quality in a fellow human being than the more commonplace assets, such as appearance, personality, and consonance with our own biases. True courage cannot be faked, so perhaps we see it as a pure test of character.

Before we elevate courage to the level of our highest values, we need to remind ourselves of the courage required of the suicide bomber, who sacrifices his or her own life in what the bomber perceives to be a higher cause. In our Western culture we associate such behavior with the insanity of religious zealotry, but from other perspectives the suicide bomber is displaying courage of a high order. We don't admire that kind of courage; in fact, we don't call it courage unless we approve of the cause for which personal sacrifices are made. Now we're in logical trouble; courage has become a soft standard, dependent on subjective values. We must ask much more of our political leaders.

## Politics

As children born in 1936 of working-class families, Pat and I were in Democratic Party childhood environments. When we reached what was then the voting age of twenty-one, however, already married, we decided that we should hear the perspectives of both parties. We flipped a coin to see who would be the family Democrat and who would be the family Republican. Both of us have changed political party affiliations more than once over the years, and neither of us can remember the results of that coin toss.

Party politics is an important element of the contemporary American political system, but political party affiliation has never been a central concern in our family. We both vote faithfully for candidates and propositions on grounds that are specific to the issues at hand, and not on the basis of political party, religion, or ideology. We search for candidates who share our values and listen carefully to arguments based on reason, always looking for political leaders who truly desire to solve problems rather than impose their ideologies.

In particular, I have resisted the use and political abuse of the labels "liberal" and "conservative." These words have meanings in the English language, by which standards I am a fiscal conservative but a liberal in human affairs, thereby creating a healthy internal tension. But in contemporary America the word "liberal" has become a disparagement and the word "conservative" a contradiction when applied to politicians who spend money irresponsibly and try to control private behavior and restrict personal freedom. What is it that they pretend to conserve? These words have lost their meaning in modern-day America. They serve primarily to divide a nation whose founding principles require coming together as one people. America's politicians in both parties have polarized the electorate in ways that threaten the core values of the American democracy.

Fortunately, the American people seem to have a great instinct for the middle way. The continuously evolving American political system has served this country well for more than two centuries. The resiliency of America's democratic form of government has been remarkable; when elected officials take America in foolish or dangerous directions, or when the extreme ends of the political spectrum become dominant in government, the tendencies of America's people to drive politicians back to the center have always prevailed. It should always be so.

Irrespective of the results of that coin toss back in 1957, Pat and I both registered as Republicans when we moved to Arizona in 1997. I had served as a university president in an advisory capacity for three Pennsylvania governors in sequence: Dick Thornburg, Bob Casey, and Tom Ridge, two Republicans and a Democrat, all three trying earnestly to meet the challenges of Pennsylvania's declining industries. Although registered as a Democrat at the time, I was proud to serve President George H. W. Bush as a member of his President's Council of Advisors on Science and Technology (PCAST) and I voted for the man as he contended unsuccessfully for his second term. When I moved to Arizona I was prepared to serve a Republican governor in collaboration with a Republican legislature. I soon realized, however, that the Arizona Republicans in power had little in common with the Republicans I had known in Pennsylvania. A few anecdotes will make the point.

My first meeting with Arizona House Speaker Jeff Groscost was a major shock. The Speaker explained to the three university presidents and the regent present that major cuts in university budgets were necessitated by the court ruling that the state must assume responsibility for the equitable provision of K-12 school buildings throughout the state, relieving school districts (and local property taxes) of this responsibility. Of course, the logical response would be to create statewide property taxes to compensate (on average) for the tax savings resulting from the local tax relief, but this option was not even under consideration in Arizona, where a two-thirds vote of the legislature is required for any tax increase. The indictment of Governor Fife Symington just as I received his nod as university president had moved Secretary of State Jane Hull into the governor's office and she tried to help, but the Speaker rejected her proposal for bond financing of the necessary capital construction, thereby necessitating cuts in General Fund budgets, most notably those of the three universities. We were stuck, he said. He saw no other options.

The meeting broke up soon after the Speaker had delivered his message, leaving me totally puzzled. Sensing my confusion as Arizona's newest university president, the Speaker's principal financial staffer, Michael Bradley, kindly took me aside to explain.

"You don't understand," he said. "The [House Republican] Caucus wants to cut your budget because you are part of government and every dollar we take away from government and give back to the people will be used more productively by them than by you."

Stunned, I cited the myriad studies of return on university investment underlying the policies of the past three Pennsylvania governors (two of them Republicans).

"I'm an economist too," said Bradley. "I can find data to prove anything."

I never figured out how to engage in productive dialogue with intelligent people who value ideological belief above informed reasoning. Adversaries who reason together can usually find their way to adequate solutions, but adversaries who replace thought by repeated recitation of dogma cannot solve problems together. One such party must win and the opponent must lose, at least until the tables are turned and power swings back to the previously defeated party. This is not the way democracy is supposed to work. Reasoned compromise is at the heart of democracy.

When scandal drove Speaker Groscost from office, I scheduled a meeting with his successor, Jim Weiers. Before I was seated comfortably in my chair, the new Speaker let me know why he did not support university budget requests.

"You are spending too much taxpayer money because you are enrolling too many students who instead ought to go out and get a job after high school like I did," said the new Speaker of the Arizona House of Representatives to the still-new president of the University of Arizona.

Some years later, after the regents had authorized the three university presidents to move their universities in different but complementary directions, I stated publicly that my first priority was to make the University of Arizona better, not bigger. When I next testified before the House Appropriations Committee, Chairman Russell Pearce welcomed me by applauding my decision to slow enrollment growth, echoing his Speaker's belief that this policy would save money. When he heard my testimony, printed for the press, he realized that I was holding the legislature accountable for systematic tax cuts that were crippling Arizona's public universities. Moreover, I was vigorously challenging the budget proposal for the coming year that he personally had floated publicly. Representative Pearce was so outraged that he didn't speak to me or shake my hand for two years. My testimony was well received by the press and by Arizona's Democratic governor, Janet Napolitano, but it was not the cautious and prudent testimony that the legislature had come to expect from Arizona's public university presidents. In the ensuing hullaballoo the outrageous budget proposal that had been advanced by the chairman of the House Appropriations Committee was properly crushed, but I paid a price. Ultimately the university may have been ill-served by my candor. Minority dissent is not graciously received in the politics of ideology.

When I retired from the university presidency in 2006 I registered as an Independent, even if Pat remained a Republican.

As the presidential election of 2008 began to dominate political thinking across the country, I focused initially on my hope that my friend and senator John McCain would receive the Republican nomination. On the Democratic side, I was sufficiently interested in Barack Obama to read his first book, which he began while still in law school. I was fascinated by every aspect of the man—his intellect, his personal story, his ideas, and his insistence on the return of civility to the American political process. I read the second book and several of his speeches with growing excitement. I began to wonder if America was ready for Barack Obama.

In Arizona, Independents can vote in either party primary, but they cannot vote at all in the "presidential preference" polls. I changed my registration to "Democrat," and voted for Barack Obama.

# 8

# Family Values

### Enduring Love

Let this story end as it began, bridging "Young Love" to "Enduring Love." Why is it that "the fiery passions of youth rarely ignite the glowing embers of enduring love"? What can young lovers learn from Pat's story and my story and our story together?

A successful, enduring marriage is most natural when both husband and wife begin their marriage feeling genuinely blessed by their good fortune in finding each other. If marriage is clouded by reservations, if it is tentative and exploratory, it will probably fail when tough times arrive, as they always do. A marriage that begins as a trial, to see how it works, will not have the strength to endure the pressures that will surely test that union. However passionately desirous of each other two young people may be, the consummation of that eager love can never be enough of a foundation on which to build an enduring marriage. Something more is needed.

But young people in love are generally not capable of the depth of feelings that come with maturity. How can they test their capacity for enduring love at a time in their lives when they cannot really know what that concept means?

The answer is simple: They must believe. They must believe to the depths of their souls that they will learn together through the decades of marriage whatever they need to know to make it work. They must have faith in themselves, faith in each other, and faith in the very concept of marriage as a lifelong union of two people forever in love.

Beyond passion and faith, they need to be tough-minded and resilient. The bonds of young love are incredibly strong, but too often they are easily fractured. An engineer would describe these bonds as strong but not tough.

My wife and I are both very tough, resilient people. As we both have demonstrated throughout our lives, we each can take a hit and keep moving forward; we can get knocked down and get up again as many times as life's fortunes demand. Our marriage has been subjected to the usual pressures of family life and perhaps a bit more, with six kids pulling us at times in different directions and sometimes down. My commitment to my job responsibilities created inevitable stresses: "What comes first, your family or your job?" But Pat and I always knew that somehow we would solve our problems together, and never apart. Confronting crises together made us stronger as individuals and as a team.

So the journey from young love to a fiftieth wedding anniversary requires both faith and tough-minded resilience, as well as the passion that brings two people together. What else is needed?

To be fair to all the people I love whose marriages have failed or who had to marry twice to find the right partner, I must acknowledge that the first thing needed for an enduring marriage is dumb luck in falling in love with the person who is right for you in the long run. When I crossed the dance floor in 1950 to meet Pat Jolley, I was not drawn to her by the quality of her character. It is sheer good luck that the girl I was attracted to then had the potential to become the woman I am in love with now, almost sixty years later.

So good luck is necessary, but it is far from sufficient. Much more is needed.

For true love to endure, the passion must never be lost. The expressions of love take changing forms, but the excitement of being together should last a lifetime.

A good marriage is founded on enduring love, but it becomes much more than that. Pat and I have always been best friends, sharing basic values and common foundations. We enjoy being together. We have become so interdependent that it is hard to imagine one without the other. As noted in the preface, that possibility was tested when on April 12, 2006, I experienced a life-threatening injury.

One hundred days after the routine placement in my chest of a pacemaker designed to establish a floor level on my heartbeat, which had always been slow, I passed out in my office at the University of Arizona and was immediately rushed to the nearby University Medical Center. Both pulse and diastolic blood pressure were undetectable for no reason that was apparent to the head of emergency medicine, Dr. Harvey

✑ *In our later years: Pat and Pete (2004). (Family photo.)*

Meislin, who was very concerned as the attending physician that day. I was unconscious and unaware that I was on the edge of death. Fortunately, Dr. Meislin listened to the suggestion of the chief resident on duty, Dr. David Gutman, who had experience with bedside emergency ultrasound equipment. They brought in the equipment, which produced a sonogram revealing the pericardial sac enveloping the heart to be filled with fluid. A big catheter needle in my chest relieved the hydraulic pressure, gave my heart room to beat, and revealed the fluid to be blood. Awake by that time and feeling the pain, I heard the doctors discussing their options.

"Open him up," said Dr. Gordon Ewy, my cardiologist. "We need to find out where that blood is coming from."

I saw my dear wife of fifty years through the glass of my examining room, and I waggled my fingers to ease the tension in her eyes. Pat was permitted to come to my side before I was wheeled off for surgery and I will always remember her parting words: "You can't go anywhere without me."

I recovered very quickly after the surgeon, Dr. Cristy Smith, opened my chest and discovered the perforation caused by the penetration of the heart wall from the inside by the lead wire of the pacemaker. It was a simple matter for an excellent surgeon to stitch that small hole closed, completely repairing the damage to my heart.

There are no lasting physical consequences of my heart injury, but the near-death experience taught me important lessons about human mortality and the proper priorities in life. I know now that, whatever the future may hold for me, whatever adversities may lie yet ahead, I have been truly blessed to find so much love in my life. Other people might measure my life by enumerating my professional achievements, but I know what really counts.

## Adversity

Why is it that adversity builds strength in some people and breaks other people completely?

Poverty was a powerful motivator for me, and Pat responded the same way. Very often, however, poverty sucks the life out of children. The differentiator, I think, is the presence or absence of hope.

When you and your family are truly destitute, feeling the need for food and shelter, you hunger for any evidence that your circumstances are temporary. If you are surrounded by people who are equally destitute, particularly in a crowded urban setting, you can easily lose hope for better times. You can easily give up on the future entirely and live from day to day in a survival mode.

In childhood Pat and I were never without food or shelter and we could always see evidence around us pointing the way to prosperity. We never doubted that we would eventually be comfortable financially, even as we made do with very little for the first ten years of our marriage, getting the education that promised relief.

What about the kid who crawls out of the deepest kind of social and financial poverty in an urban ghetto and climbs to the top of his or her field, with commensurate reward? What makes this person different? Is there always a good mama in the home, or someone to guide the way? Or is there something in the biological makeup of that extraordinary person that enables first survival and then success? I don't know the answer.

The question is important because it reaches beyond poverty to all kinds of adversity. If we knew the answers we would be better parents, shaping our children's early experiences to give them the strength to deal with later adversities.

I do believe that we can all better cope with adversity by keeping our problems in perspective. It helps to have an example in mind of a fellow human being who has managed adversity with special courage and exceptional grace. Nelson Mandela comes to mind if you search for a world leader who overcame adversities that seemed overwhelming. If you search within your own personal relationships you can find your own immediate examples. I've mentioned Cheri Blauwet, the girl from Iowa whose wheelchair has not slowed her down. In my own family I think of Bee Jolley, Pat's brother.

Bee's military career included a stint as a paratrooper and many years flying helicopters and fixed-wing military aircraft. In Vietnam he dropped his helicopter into many firefights, taking hits and losing buddies but somehow surviving. He retired after twenty years and joined his family in Alaska, where he became a bush pilot, flying equipment and supplies into the backcountry. Landing on a dry streambed with fifty-gallon drums of gasoline on board, he hit soft sand and flipped his airplane. He had the presence of mind to turn off the ignition as he landed upside down, before he broke his neck in the crash.

Bee was rescued by the pilot of a second airplane on this run, but he arrived at the hospital in Anchorage paralyzed from the neck down. Bee refused to accept the doctors' prognosis of permanent paralysis and arranged a transfer to Seattle's Veterans Hospital, where after very extensive surgery he regained some feeling in his limbs. After months of painful therapy, he walked out of that hospital, still a quadriplegic because he is impaired to some degree throughout his body, but not totally incapacitated and still undaunted.

Bee recovered sufficiently to teach ROTC for a time in an Anchorage high school and coach the rifle team to a state championship.

The twenty years since his accident have taken their toll, and Bee is in his wheelchair for most of his waking hours now, but he has faced staggering adversity with quite remarkable equanimity and good humor. He enjoys his music and his family in good spirits and without complaint.

If I ever begin to feel overcome by my own adversities, I think about Bee Jolley.

🙠 *Bee Jolley in high school (1960) and at home (2006),* undaunted and par-
tially recovered after his paralyzing plane injury. *(School and family photos.)*

## Family Values

The phrase "family values" has a comforting ring to it. Unfortunately,
this phrase has been effectively co-opted by politicians who have used
it to identify the values of a certain kind of idealized family, one very
different from mine. I would like to see that wonderful combination of
good words, "family values," become more broadly understood.

Many Americans, especially older Americans of European stock,
remember a small-town childhood in the 1950s, living in a community
that was safe and predictable, a place where no one locked the doors
at night and everyone felt comfortable letting their kids have the run of
the town all day long, and even into the evening hours. They remember
as kids feeling free and at the same time protected. They knew that the
neighbors were watching out for them even if their parents were not
around, and they also knew that they couldn't get away with anything

because those same neighbors would tell their folks if they broke the rules, which were pretty much the same for every family. Usually the dads went off to work at the beginning of the day, but the moms stayed home and watched out for each other's kids. Grandparents were often in the same neighborhood, creating warm memories of special holidays or just a comforting presence in childhood. Families could afford to make do with one paycheck, in part because their sense of what they had to have was modest. Prayer, thrift, and honest labor made these communities work, and we remember them fondly.

Many Americans who experienced those emotionally comfortable times look back with a sense of loss, knowing that those close communities in America are rapidly disappearing. They may see the past as a kind of golden age in their own lives, the source of their most basic values, which they may think of as "family values."

Pat and I share many of these memories and also find them comforting. I was raised by a single mother who had to go to work every day, but I lived in a cabin with no locks on the doors and enjoyed the utter freedom of entire days with no restrictions as I hiked, swam, and caroused with my buddies in Paradise Park. However, I also have memories of those times that are not so wonderful. I am not alone in these darker memories of the 1950s, but the culture of those times did not encourage talking about family problems to people outside of the immediate family.

Fortunately for our mental health, human beings have a wonderful capacity to bury the bad memories and cherish the good. We can easily forget that the America of the 1950s, which we have idealized as a time of beautiful families, was also a time when men could abuse their wives and children and keep it in the family, free from intervention by the authorities. We forget, or never really knew, that this golden era offered few opportunities for women or people of color. We tend to look past the dark side of our childhood lives.

Pat is a member of the Santa Cruz High School graduating class of 1954, which has become very close in recent years because of Internet communications and frequent reunions. The class president remembered feeling as a high school student very much alone in his misery as part of a dysfunctional family, and he asked his classmates by e-mail to tell their own stories of family strife, now that after more than fifty years their parents would no longer be alarmed by the telling of family secrets. We were all surprised to discover that many apparently well-adjusted classmates were struggling secretly at home in families badly damaged by alcoholism, abuse, parental infidelity, or other forms of trauma. In our seventies we are all survivors who can look back upon these trials with some good humor, but we do have to admit that family life was not always as good as we tried to make it appear in the fifties.

Although rumors of scandalous behavior could move through those small towns like wildfire, most folks minded their own business, so people could stay close without conflict. One of the reasons people were so close with their neighbors was the longevity of relationships. People usually stayed in the town where they were born, and often in the same neighborhood. Moreover, the neighbors all looked alike. If the family next door was not actually related by birth, it may as well have been. "Family values" extended beyond the limits of the biological families, but the extended family showed signs of the same genealogical heritage.

These communities broke down for a reason. Their young people (and some daring older people) decided that they could find greater opportunity elsewhere. Their success was contagious, and others followed. People left these comfortable homes because they wanted to.

Financial opportunity and a sense of adventure created a generation of mobile Americans, some of them first tasting the world outside of their hometowns in military service and some in college, but all in a common search for a better place. We should not look back upon this phenomenon as some kind of decline, but as evidence of the spirit of Americans in a new generation.

An inevitable consequence of population mobility is interaction among people of different heritages and traditions. Military service requires such interactions, although individuals in the military are usually free to associate socially with people with similar background and ethnicity. In college life, however, cultures intermingle with few inhibitions and significant effect. Young people fall in love, perhaps to marry, perhaps to make babies; boundaries based on religion or race or language or ethnicity disappear as a biological imperative. The result is a social stratification that is more driven by education and financial status than by race or religion or ethnicity. This is a new America.

My family is a reflection of that new America, but we still embrace many of the traditional family values. We think that we have added some values that are just as basic to decent family living as those that we inherited. We have rejected some of the traditional values, such as those that made a man's home his castle, where he could reign supreme, unchecked by any interfering laws. There are no conditions and no limit to the love that Pat and I share in our marriage; our commitment to marital fidelity is stronger than the actuality of the 1950s. We work hard, live modestly, and take care of our extended families. Whereas wayward children and unwed teenage mothers were often rejected by the families of the 1950s, we don't give up on our kids, who are assured of our unconditional love even in the most dire circumstances. We go to church every week, contribute to charitable causes, volunteer in our community, and live by the common virtues that define the term "family values" as understood in America. We believe that the best of America's family values can be preserved in the new America, but only if the concept of "family" is permitted to take on a new meaning. If Americans can learn to embrace the diversity of the American people and extend the concept of family to be more inclusive, the old virtues worth keeping can live in this new world. If not, then not.

## A Woman's Place

The traditional concept of family in America relies upon some assumptions about the role of women that are incompatible with reality in the twenty-first century. These assumptions include the relegation of all women to supportive roles in our society, and that is neither fair to women nor wise in the utilization of human resources for the benefit of society.

In twenty-first-century America a woman's place is wherever her desires, efforts, capabilities, and opportunities take her. For some women (and some men) the best place is in "the home," as was widely assumed for all women in the 1950s, but this cannot ever again be the presumption of our society. Those days are gone forever.

Many Americans who approve wholeheartedly of the increased opportunities becoming available for women in our society still disapprove of the changing attitudes toward women's sexuality. Because we rarely examine the attitudes toward male sexuality that were already deeply embedded in our culture in the 1950s, we often decry as new phenomena the prominence of sexual imagery in contemporary culture and the sexual promiscuity we unleashed in the 1960s. It may seem that we have liberated the sexuality specifically of women, but in truth we have also liberated the suppressed sexuality of men. How do we get that genie back in the bottle?

If ever we are going to find our way to a healthy societal attitude toward human sexuality, we must get there not by going backwards to the male-dominated norms of the 1950s, but by going forward to an era in which both men and women are expected to contribute to a societal perspective on acceptable sexual behavior.

The use of the phrase "women's liberation" to describe the changing role of women in our society can be misleading. My mother was "liberated" when she was abandoned by her first husband and obliged to get a job, and then when she was thrust into the role of business owner/operator when her second husband died. She managed her small business well and prospered as an example for other women to emulate, but I don't think she felt "liberated." She just did what she had to do, as did thousands of women in similar circumstances.

A myriad of forces are at work in the evolution of society. The deliberate stimuli of the "thought leaders" of the 1960s were important, of course, but it is difficult to sort out causes of social change. Many women were driven into the workforce by the "invisible hand" of a changing economy, and they soon realized that education and job training were the keys to success in this arena as we moved into a knowledge-based, global economy.

Before long, women were earning the majority of bachelor's degrees in American colleges and universities, and soon thereafter the majority of master's degrees. Doctoral degrees may well be next. In the formerly male-dominated colleges of medicine and law, women are also moving to majority status. Moreover, the learning experiences of women are also changing in qualitative ways, as indicated by new leadership in campus politics and new prominence in intercollegiate athletics. The consequences of this ascension of women in higher education are easy to anticipate in this increasingly knowledge-based society.

Slowly, college and university faculty are also changing, most dramatically in the ranks of assistant professors and the presidents and chancellors of our colleges and universities. At this writing, half of the Ivy League presidents are women (one a black woman) and women now lead three of America's most prominent historically technological universities (MIT, Rensselaer Polytechnic Institute, and Lehigh), again one a black woman. This was unimaginable twenty years ago.

The implications of the changing role of women in American institutions of higher education are almost certain to be profound in all leadership roles in our society: business, politics, religion, entertainment, arts, the professions, and government at all levels.

This is a good thing for America; we need all the help we can get.

But what about the family? How can women take their rightful place among the leaders in American society without damaging the family?

The biological role of females as child-bearers cannot be shared with males. Human biology assigns to mothers of infants a different role than fathers can be expected to play, and in varying degrees these differences persist over the early years of a child's life. How can we develop healthy family values if America's children see their mothers and fathers mostly when they're racing off to work in the morning or dragging home weary at the end of the day?

If both grandparents are also still committed to their work lives or living far away, as is often the case today, the challenges of raising small children with the right values are compounded. Parents and grandparents are all very important people in the life of a child.

This dilemma, the search for a healthy balance between family commitments and the need to meet responsibilities outside the home, has no easy resolution. In fact, we didn't often get it right in the 1950s either, with Mom stuck in the house and Dad totally committed to his own work (or occasional play). Every family needs to work hard to achieve the combination of work, play, and family life that is right for them. Keeping the marriage intact is an important first step. Achieving the right balance may require a family support system that extends beyond the conventional boundaries of "family."

Pat and I found the balance that worked for us in raising our six children and some of the grandchildren who followed.

## Grandchildren

"How many grandchildren do you have?"

This is a natural question to ask of Pat and me, septuagenarians with six and then five grown children and more than fifty years of marriage together. It's one of those friendly and courteous questions that people ask in the expectation of a simple, numerical answer; they don't really want to hear a lengthy discourse on what it means to be a grandparent. So I usually just say "Eight," and ask my questioner about her family, or his.

What I really want to say is, "Who counts as a grandchild?"

Do the two children born to Lora's second husband in a previous marriage count as our grandchildren? They call us Nana and Grandpa and they are loved as family. They do count for Pat and me.

What about the child our son John conceived when he was seventeen? She is loved by us as family, even if she has been raised (beautifully)

*❧ Pete with granddaughter Paige Lieberman, born to John and adopted by Molly and Mike Lieberman (2009). (Family photo.)*

as the adopted daughter of family friends, Molly and Mike Lieberman. Yes, she is our granddaughter too.

Of course Tom counts. Maybe he counts twice, once as our daughter Teresa's birth child and again as our daughter Lora's adopted son.

Krista gave birth to two children, Christian and Carly, so of course they count as our grandchildren. Their adoptions by my niece Jennifer and her husband, Mike Swansen, make Christian and Carly the grandchildren also of my sister Katy, Jennifer's mother, so we are related to these two children twice.

Linda bore two children, Xavier and Felicity, to a man she never married. They also count as our grandchildren.

That makes eight grandchildren by our count, but Pat and I count in funny ways. Because all of our children are adopted, we don't think in terms of "blood relatives." We think in terms of relationships.

I will spare my grandchildren further description of their generation, young people whose lives are just now unfolding, except to make the

⌁ Above: Grandson Tom (c. 1994), born to Teresa and adopted by Lora. (School photo.)

⌁ Right: Grandson Tom and daughter Krista with Norwegian elkhound Loki (2009). (Family photo.)

⌁ Left: Grandchildren Carly and Christian (2004), born to Krista, adopted by Michael and Jennifer Swansen. (Family photo.)

observation that in every case race is ambiguous for children born to my children. Classifying and categorizing my six children in racial terms is not always easy, but the rather arbitrary "rules" of our society do provide labels for each of them. There are no rules for classifying some of my grandchildren, whose physical appearance and habits of speech show no evidence of their biological heritage. Christian Swansen looks more like his Danish/Polish American adopted father, his only "real" father, than he looks like his birth mother, who is easily classified as an African American despite a biological heritage more European than African. Who labels Christian?

If these observations about our grandchildren were nothing more than further evidence of the peculiarities of my family, there would be no point in telling this story. But similar stories are being played out all over America all the time, with accelerating consequences that must be recognized if our social fabric is to hold together.

Interracial children have been part of the American story since the first Europeans came to this country, initially as male adventurers who left Indian women with babies and later as plantation owners who fathered children with their black slaves. The mores of society suppressed the conscious recognition of this reality for generations, but there can be no more silence on this subject in the new America that is emerging today. A large but undefined percentage of the American citizenry could claim more than one race in their genealogy if they chose to do so. Census takers tell us that this category, "more than one race," is the fastest-growing sector of the American population in percentage terms, presumably because more and more Americans are so identifying themselves. We are going to have to recognize the complexities of race relations in America, moving past polarization to a more nuanced understanding of contemporary reality. We will be obliged to accept the American population as a continuum of the world's peoples, not just a collection of human islands of race. If we are wise, we will learn to recognize this reality as a great strength of the United States in the eyes of the world.

Yes, this new America will be a better place for my grandchildren. It will be a better place for your grandchildren too.

## The Inclusive Family

Lora's second marriage ceremony was held in our Tucson home. Pat and I walked together with Lora down an improvised aisle. Pat was there, of course, as Lora's mother. But Lora's birth mother, Carol Signet, was also there, with her husband. Lora's birth father, Bob Barker, was there with his family too. The groom, Frank Woods, had fewer parents to bring to the affair, but he had two children by his first marriage in attendance. Of course, Lora's son Tom was there. Lora's siblings and Frank's siblings were well represented. All of these people are included in our family.

An outsider might see the Likins family as an anomaly, an example that is curious, perhaps, but not relevant to other families. We see our family as a model of inclusivity that might be embraced as an American ideal. Is that naive? Can the world really work that way? Can it really be true that other American families have complicated lives too, some like ours and others unique to their own circumstances, but all creating the kind of stresses that fall naturally from the complexities of modern life? Might our story have application to their stories?

This book is written at one point in time about my own family, but our stories are shared with other families all over America. My family will continue to evolve, as all families do, with births and deaths, marriage and divorce, and changing relationships, but the root story shared with other American families will remain.

As must be obvious by now, my concept of family has fuzzy boundaries. You cannot easily count its members. It grows not only internally by virtue of new births but externally by familial associations. It may get smaller by voluntary withdrawal, but not by ejection from within. It is not diminished by divorce or by the death of a family member.

Core values bind my family together, but different ones among us have different opinions about many important matters, and that's okay.

We are not all the same color, not all the same size, and not all the same in our personal aspirations and ambitions. We're not all equally smart in an academic way and not all equally smart in our street skills. That's okay, as long as we respect each other and play fair.

We're not all equally nice all the time; in fact we have all made mistakes and none of us is as nice as we want to be all the time. But we forgive and come together again.

In these chaotic times, filled with uncertainties and anxieties about unknown dangers, it is very important to have some kind of foundation on which to stand with confidence, some kind of rock to cling to when storms gather. It is very important to have a family, even if you have to invent one yourself.

## An All American Family

The top eight wrestlers in each weight class of the annual NCAA Wrestling Tournament are celebrated as "all-Americans." In many collegiate sports the same phrase is used to designate individuals in the very highest echelon of their sports.

Note the hyphen in "all-Americans." Not every all-American wrestler is a U.S. citizen; Japanese nationals in American universities are fully eligible, and some have emerged not only as all-Americans but as gold-medal champions. In swimming, track, baseball, basketball, soccer, gymnastics, tennis, golf, and virtually every other sport, American universities have recruited top athletes from all over the world who have succeeded at the highest level, all-Americans who are not all Americans.

The children in my family, who cannot pretend to the highest echelon of American youth by the standards of athletics or academics or creative artistry or entrepreneurship or any other conventional category of performance, are nonetheless all Americans, all born in this country and representative of the diversity of the American population. America is changing demographically at accelerating speed, and the old stereotype of the American family, the Anderson family of television's *Father Knows Best* in the middle to late fifties, must give way to a new model.

Does it seem presumptuous for me to suggest that my own family somehow typifies the emerging new model of an American family? Our family life has been complicated by schizophrenia, drug addiction, unwed pregnancy, divorce, adoption, homosexuality, interreligious marriage, and the complexities of race and ethnicity in America. We have also celebrated high achievement in academic, athletic, and financial terms, and shared a lot of love. Does all of this somehow add up to span the range of experiences of American families today?

There is no available statistical basis for answering this question, but my own very public experience with my family suggests that all my family characteristics are more common in contemporary America than the innocent might imagine.

After John's death Pat and I were asked to speak to medical students at the University of Arizona by a professor who wanted to humanize his lectures on mental illness. We've been talking to these young people once a year for perhaps five years.

We co-chaired a fund-raising walk for the National Alliance on Mental Illness here in Tucson, and after a luncheon address I was asked to share my experiences in a class for law enforcement officers who were developing new approaches for dealing with street people. I've been participating in these courses now for several years.

Whether I'm talking to docs or cops, I always ask the same question: "Do you have any experience with addiction or any other mental illness in your family, including the generations from grandparents to grandchildren?" Roughly half the medical students raised their hands immediately. Law enforcement officers are more reticent, reluctant to admit weakness in the family, but with a little encouragement half of those in attendance typically respond affirmatively too. Mental illness is more prevalent than we like to believe. We compound the stigma by suppressing or denying this aspect of our lives.

Similarly, we need to acknowledge that the statistics about unwed mothers derive from our own families, not from some invisible "others" in our society.

As our friends and family members "come out of the closet," we are discovering gays and lesbians among us. In my youth, in the 1950s, these people were mostly invisible, but their apparent rarity was an illusion.

Racial heritage was not always acknowledged in the 1950s by those who could "pass" as members of the majority, despite the consequent psychological burden. Interracial relationships were often hidden. Today it seems that most extended families in America include more than one race.

Religious boundaries are also breaking down for couples whose religious traditions cannot keep them apart.

With all this understood, my family seems more normal and perhaps even typical of the emerging norms for American families. With all our problems, our weaknesses as well as our strengths, ours is becoming the all American family of the twenty-first century. Are you ready for this?

 The Likins kids in our first year together (1972). Clockwise from
top: John, Teresa, Lora, Paul, Linda, and Krista. (Family photo.)

➤ *The Likins family (1983). Top row (left to right): Lora, Pete, Pat, and Teresa; bottom row (left to right): John, Linda, Krista, and Paul, with Norwegian elkhound Smokey. (*Bethlehem Globe-Times *photo, December 18, 1983; used by permission of the* Express-Times.*)*

# Index of Names

# About the Author

Peter Likins describes himself in the preface to *A New American Family* as "an old white guy . . . a straight, Catholic, former Republican trained as an engineer." He may seem an unlikely author for an emotional book about a family highlighting six children adopted from many strands of the American tapestry, woven together as "an American family." But he is the father of that family, and this says more about him than can be found in his professional résumé. His marriage to Patricia well over fifty years ago is an important clue to the reconciliation of his personal story with his formal record, which can be rather intimidating.

Educated through the Ph.D. at Stanford, MIT, and Stanford again, Likins became a spacecraft engineer working on problems of dynamics and control, beginning at the Caltech Jet Propulsion Laboratory in 1958 (the year JPL orbited America's first successful Earth satellite). For a dozen years on the UCLA engineering faculty he was engaged in teaching and research in these fields, earning recognition as a Fellow of the American Institute of Aeronautics and Astronautics and subsequent election to the National Academy of Engineering.

Moving to Columbia University as dean of engineering and applied science and then provost of the university, he advanced after six years to the presidency of Lehigh University, where he served for fifteen years before accepting the presidency of the University of Arizona, retiring after nine years at the age of seventy.

Somewhere along the way he was elected to the National Wrestling Hall of Fame in its Hall of Outstanding Americans.

All academics publish extensively and Likins is responsible for scores of research publications and three books, authored or co-authored as engineering textbooks or research monographs. Never before has he published anything comparable to *A New American Family*.